WORKING TOGETHER

The Art of Consulting & Communicating

by

Anita DeBoer

ISBN 1-57035-041-8

Edited by Bill Tosh
Text layout and design by Susan Krische
Cover design by Londerville Design

Printed in the United States of America

Published and Distributed by

SOPRIS
WEST
EDUCATIONAL SERVICES

A Cambium Learning™ Company

4093 Specialty Place • Longmont, Colorado 80504 • (303) 651-2829
www.sopriswest.com

71WORK/3-05

Anita DeBoer is a speaker, author, and professional development facilitator/teacher in the areas of collaboration, consultation, co-teaching, communication skills, coaching, conflict management, change, and effective instructional practices. Anita travels extensively throughout North America and overseas teaching and studying these areas. She is a former university professor, consulting teacher, general education teacher, special education teacher (students with learning disabilities, behavioral disorders, and mental retardation), parent educator, and recreational therapist (at an institution for people with mental and physical disabilities). Dr. DeBoer has written a book, a precursor to *Working Together*, entitled *The Art of Consulting*, authored several articles related to collaboration, co-produced a video on collaborative problem solving, and is currently co-authoring a book entitled *Strategies & Tools for Collaborative Teaching*. The latter contains many planning tools that make collaborative efforts among teachers more efficient and effective. Currently, Anita lives in Florida and her interests include writing, politics, art, flower gardening, downhill skiing, in-line skating, her husband, Gerry, and her daughter, Carolyn.

To my daughter, Carolyn, whom I am constantly trying to emulate. She is what I hope some day to become. And to the memory of my daughter, Janet, who taught me so much about living and dying in her eight short years.

This book has a long ancestry; many people and experiences have shaped my thinking over the years. To properly, completely, and adequately acknowledge each person whose influence has found its way into this book is impossible. However, there are a few dear friends who deserve special mention: Marilee Ciello, whose confidence in my ability to both speak and write has been constant over the years. She unselfishly gives both her time and energy when I need it. Catherine Pidek is a continual source of intellectual stimulation. Her constructive feedback always gives me the courage to continue. Susan Fister, whose contribution is hard to put into words, but whose influence and support are immeasurable.

To others who have left their mark on these pages because of long conversations we have had about consulting and communicating effectively, I extend my appreciation. They are Daena Richmond, Candice Barels, John Richards, Judith Kern-Bertrum, Veronica Hooker, Randy Cranston, and Judith King.

As importantly, I want to acknowledge all my consultees, past and present, without whom I could not have done my work or written this book. They continue to facilitate my growth through their unrelenting curiosity about how they can become the best they are capable of being. Unknowingly, they are my teachers. Thank you all for your tremendous contribution to my life and work.

Finally, I want to extend my appreciation and love to my husband, Gerry, for his encouragement to first write, then rewrite, this book. His belief in me is unwavering.

*J*ust when you think you know how this thing called consulting and collaborating works, the rules change. I did not set out to change the rules. I set out on a journey to discover what working together could look and sound like in the future. I also set out to understand the practice of consulting from a general educator's point of view. This perspective was very enlightening. I soon realized that consulting does not have to be conceptualized the way it usually is. Consultants need not be a limited pool of specialists working with a large pool of teachers, typically referred to as consultees. These roles can be reciprocal. That is, teachers can function as co-consultants by pooling their interdisciplinary content knowledge, processes, and expertise (Phillips & McCullough, 1990). It can be argued that we will need all the consultants we can get if we are to be successful with the ever increasing challenges in our future. In addition, we need to value the "special" knowledge each of us has regarding curriculum, instruction, assessment, classroom management, and individual differences in learning and behaving. The outcomes of such an endeavor can be learning environments that are exciting, challenging, productive, and fulfilling places for everyone to be: teachers, students, administrators, and parents alike.

Fullan & Hargreaves (1991) remind us of the difficulty of establishing collaborative work cultures when they say, "There is simply not enough opportunity and not enough encouragement for teachers to work together, learn from each other, and improve their expertise as a community" (p. 1).

We also know that there is not enough user-friendly information or enough professional development for teachers to learn the skills necessary for collaborating, consulting, and communicating with colleagues. Thus, the reason for this book.

Working Together: The Art of Consulting & Communicating describes how educators can design and engage in peer or collegial problem solving as one way to learn and grow professionally. It describes and helps develop the essential skills that educators will need when working together: trust-building, listening, facilitating, collaborating, questioning, communicating, and peer problem solving. It also describes several interactive strategies that allow people to be proactive, not just reactive, with conflict.

I tried to make the contents of this book clear and practical. I have drawn extensively from my own experiences as a consulting teacher. The information you will read is the outgrowth of 25 years of observing, studying, and interviewing people interacting in their workplace. The unique perspective and collective wisdom of classroom teachers has heavily influenced my thinking over the years.

The style of this book is not academic, although it is based on scores of research studies and a multitude of conversations with people who consult with colleagues every day. For ease of reading, I have not heavily referenced the text nor have I discussed the outstanding and important work of my colleagues. The sources utilized are provided in the reference list. My foremost objective was to produce a thoughtful, reader-friendly guide for educators who either want to develop or need to reflect on their skills for consulting and communicating effectively with colleagues.

A major purpose of this book is to provide information that would allow people to celebrate the strengths that they bring to a collaborative relationship, as well as to become aware of how they might unknowingly contribute to an unproductive working experience with some colleagues. The information will also allow people to reflect on what makes their consulting efforts so successful at times, as well as what makes them so difficult and challenging at other times. This book focuses on three big areas: (1) a way to consult with colleagues, that is, a problem-solving process; (2) the communication skills we use when we consult, that is, our skills for listening to and speaking with peers; and (3) our styles of behaving, that is, the way we tend to do things—our habits.

Chapter 1 begins with an overview of consulting. It reviews past practices and suggests strategies for expanding the use of consulting as a peer-learning model. Chapter 2 describes a comprehensive problem-solving process that you can adopt or adapt when consulting with colleagues. Chapter 3 explores the strengths and limitations of three interactive approaches for consulting: facilitative, collaborative, and authoritative. Chapters 4 and 5 review the communication skills you will need if consulting is to be all that it should be. Chapters 6 and 7 describe the wide range of interpersonal styles— the glasses through which we view our world. Chapter 8 explains in detail how we can work effectively with people who have different interpersonal styles. The final chapters, 9 and 10, examine those issues that make consulting with peers successful and those that make it difficult and challenging.

Finally, let me make one point even more explicit. The survival of our planet will be determined by the way in which nations and people work together to create a more promising future for us and our children. The future of our schools is contingent upon educators working and consulting with one another about work-related issues. Sarason (1990) says it best:

> . . . for our schools to do better than they do we have to give up the belief that it is possible to create the conditions for productive learning when those conditions do not exist for educational personnel (p. 13). ❧

Productive learning occurs when educators work together to create new visions, analyze important issues, design options, evaluate outcomes, and reflect on their practices. The skills of teaching and the needs of students today and in the future are too complex to go it alone. We need to develop partnerships and share the journey with people traveling in the same direction. We do not all need to be on the same road; through our collaborative efforts we may find that many different roads can take us to our destination.

Enjoy!

contents

chapter 10

DIFFICULT CONSULTING **195**

What makes it challenging? What should I pay more attention to?

1

WHATEVER YOU DO IN LIFE, DO IT WITH ENTHUSIASM.

CONSULTING

What it is.
What it can be.

ou cannot pick up a professional journal, a business magazine, or listen to a discussion on international politics without noting the emphasis placed on people working collaboratively. Collaboration is believed to be a main ingredient for change because it allows people to reflect on their practice together and, as a result, to grow professionally. It also allows people to solve problems that they were unlikely to solve on their own and to collectively design strategies for creating a better tomorrow. There are many structures for collaboration; consulting is one of them. Others include peer coaching, co-teaching, student support teams, peer collaboration, and interdisciplinary teaming.

For years, professions such as medicine and law have consulted with colleagues about difficult work related problems. It is general practice for doctors to learn their profession through ongoing shared experiences. More recently, the educational community has awakened to the benefits of working cooperatively and collaboratively. The strategies range from cooperative learning for students to co-consulting for adults.

The word *consulting* causes apprehension for many educators because most of us do not see ourselves in that capacity, but the truth is that we consult every day although we may not call it as such. Either we consult with someone or someone consults with us about an issue, problem, concern, or to just get the information we need. The people with whom we consult on a regular basis are spouses, friends, doctors, lawyers, tax consultants, hair stylists, parents, and/or colleagues. Hence, the roles of a consultant or a consultee are not unfamiliar to us. We are already doing them!

As professionals, it is refreshing to openly approach colleagues who have varied expertise and training to obtain their insights and ideas about problems we are facing, or to discuss how to implement a program. Typically, when we consult with colleagues, it is done in an informal manner; it is spontaneous and unscheduled. It is also nonsystematic in that we do not adhere to any formal or organized process during our discussion. If we were to use a more explicit problem-solving or planning process when discussing work related problems, the outcomes could be even more beneficial.

People who consult regularly with colleagues believe that the experience is both exhilarating and challenging. It is exhilarating because it is such an incredible learning opportunity. It may, in fact, be one of the best forms of professional development available to educators. Rarely will you consult with someone, either as the consultant or consultee, and not feel that you have learned something new. Sometimes you will develop new teaching and learning strategies and other times you will learn a great deal about human behavior, especially your own. In addition, at times you will learn what a challenge it is to work with people who are not like you! To work effectively with people who are not like you requires a deep understanding of the relationship between interactive communication skills and interpersonal styles.

Generally, when we consult with friends or colleagues, we use a variety of interactive approaches and we expect that they will also use a variety of approaches when they consult with us. For example, there are times when we want a colleague to just listen to us and provide feedback as we talk aloud about work related concerns. At other times we want a colleague to think aloud along with us about how to implement a particular program, such as cooperative learning. There are also times when we want a colleague to provide us with critical information in response to a direct question such as, "What is thematic instruction all about?" The key to successful consulting relationships is being aware of the different approaches and using them flexibly and appropriately. Chapter 3 focuses exclusively on the skills and benefits of each interactive approach.

Similarly, when we consult with friends or colleagues, we find that they have different interpersonal styles than we do. They behave and think differently from us. Some people are high risk takers, while others proceed more cautiously. Some people are very people oriented, while others function more independently. Higher risk takers are generally those people who are first to implement a new practice. Those who are more cautious tend to stand by, watch, and analyze the consequences. Then, when it seems right and comfortable to do so, they implement something new. Individuals who are very people oriented love to work and interact frequently with colleagues. Those who are more independent tend to work in relative isolation from their peers. Fortunately or unfortunately, depending upon your point of view, an increasing part of our daily routine as educators requires that we work with people who differ from us on these personal dimensions. Because of its importance, three chapters of this book are dedicated solely to understanding interpersonal styles: yours and the people with whom you interact throughout your life.

The majority of times we consult with friends or colleagues it works well, we feel good about it, and we get what we need. Yet, there are other times we leave the situation feeling frustrated that our time has been wasted. The information in this book will help in understanding what elements are present when the process is working for everyone as well as in identifying how we unknowingly obstruct the process at times. You will learn an array of strategies related to the *art* of consulting and communication. The art involves the development of human relationship skills that will increase your effectiveness both as a consultant and consultee in any problem-solving and planning situation.

WHAT CONSULTING IS

Consulting is one of many interactive structures that people use to grow professionally and make changes in their workplace. As such, it is a way to develop a supportive work culture where there is mutual trust and respect among colleagues as well as continuous opportunities for life-long learning. These elements are essential if we are to adjust to the constant, rapid changes in our work and home environments.

Consulting, when it is done *formally* in an educational environment, involves a process for guided discussion that allows individuals with different talents, backgrounds, styles, and experiences to plan effective strategies that will achieve clearly defined outcomes. The outcomes may involve changes in people (students and teachers) and/or changes in the organization. In principle and often in practice, the process is collaborative in nature; that is, there is joint responsibility and interdependence for achieving the desired outcomes.

Consulting has been described by Peter Block as "an act of service in which consultants are expected to help achieve ends that are determined by the client. . . . It is a learn-as-you-go, create together process" (Sparks, 1992, p. 12). What this suggests is that no amount of training can prepare you for every type of problem or person you will encounter. While training is important, you do not really learn how to consult effectively until you do it again and again. Repeated and ongoing practice is what helps you master the *how* of consulting.

Lippit & Lippit (1978) describe consulting as "a two-way interaction—a process of seeking, giving, and receiving help. Consulting is aimed at aiding a person, group, organization, or larger system in mobilizing internal and external resources to deal with problem confrontation and change efforts (p. 1)."

Lippitt & Lippitt (1978) also say that consultants can play a number of roles along a continuum, from directive to nondirective; from an information expert to a joint problem solver to an objective observer/reflector.

Successful consulting always has two distinct, but mutually supportive elements: (1) a problem-solving or planning process and (2) effective communication skills. In many ways, successful consulting is like a great tapestry. Their similarity is that they both have a warp and a weft that need to be artfully woven together if the intended results are to be realized. One can envision the warp in consulting to be the problem-solving stages, while the weft represents the communication skills that need to be woven throughout the problem-solving or planning process. In both instances, if either the warp or the weft is missing, all you have is a lot of string hanging loose and you will not experience the results you want. In other words, if either efficient problem-solving or the communication skills that help you relate to people are missing, you are unlikely to experience the results you want. Both are essential!

Consulting is a way for two people or a team to generate ideas together. Either two professionals can meet and plan or a school-based team can be designed to address school-related problems. Each arrangement has its positive and negative elements. Some advantages for the dyad are:

♦ It is easier to schedule a meeting when only two people are involved.

♦ The consultee is likely to be much more actively involved in the process than when more people are present.

♦ With fewer professionals, the process is less unwieldy.

Advantages of the dyad are obvious when you think about it this way: It is difficult to be left out of a pair and active involvement enhances one's commitment. Some advantages for team consulting are:

♦ The "group brain" can generate more ideas.

♦ The wider range of expertise among colleagues generates ideas that are disparate in nature.

♦ Diverse skills yields more powerful results (Phillips & McCullough, 1992).

How does one decide whether to consult in a dyad or in a team? That decision depends upon the problem or issue at hand. A guideline to follow is: The problem should be matched to the amount of resources and expertise needed to solve it (West & Idol,

1990). The best practice is to start small and add professionals only as needed to solve the problem. For example, a fourth grade teacher consults with a colleague and during problem discovery both realize that the strategies they need to achieve their goals require the expertise of other professionals. They then invite these particular professionals into the discussion.

WHAT CONSULTING IS NOT

There are many mistaken beliefs and questionable practices related to consulting. Due to this fact, people may be apprehensive about its use and, as a result, consulting will not be perceived as a viable or valuable professional development structure. The following are some of the abuses to the practice.

Contrary to how it is often practiced, consulting is *not* simply an opportunity to give advice wherein one person says, "Tell me what to do," and the other person foolishly does so *before* the nature of the problem is clarified to the satisfaction of the person seeking information (i.e., the problem initiator). In other words, a consultant does not use this opportunity to jump in early and drop his or her pearls of wisdom on his or her co-worker and then expect a follow through without question or ongoing support following the initial meeting. Usually we do not want advice from colleagues, even when we ask for it—at least not right away. Think about when you visit your doctor. The last thing you want him or her to do is write a prescription (a solution) if you do not believe that he or she has listened to you explain your symptoms in sufficient detail and empathized to some degree with your pain. Listening to the person's feelings and acknowledging the complexity of the problem should precede any discussion of possible solutions if the consulting process is going to benefit everyone involved.

Another common error made by consultants is to feel that it is *solely* their responsibility to find answers for other people. This approach is naive, unwise, and demeaning to the person seeking support. The approach should be more collaborative in nature. There should be joint responsibility between consultant and consultee for problem finding, development of an intervention plan, and discussion of the tasks involved for implementing and evaluating the plan. An effective approach that endures over time is one that helps people find their *own* answers to *their* problems. For this to happen, a consultant needs to play an active, facilitating role, not simply one of an answer giver. This concept is not new. The argument for this approach was first stated by Galileo when he said, "You cannot teach a man anything, you can only help him discover it for himself." More recently, the work of Pugach & Johnson (1988a, 1988b, 1988c) has shown that professionals with similar expertise (e.g., pairs of general educators) can guide their peers to develop their own solutions to problems through the use of a highly-structured planning process.

Effective consulting should not depend solely upon informal planning (unguided discussion), unscheduled meetings (catch them when you can), or memos (often not acknowledged) among the individuals involved. For maximum effectiveness, professional dialogue should be guided by a process, scheduled during work hours, and involve face-to-face interaction.

Consulting is *more* than just nondirective communication or a counseling session where a person unloads his problems or vents her anger, but no action plan is developed. When it is perceived or conducted in such a manner, it does the process a great injustice. Although both of the aforementioned elements are involved to some degree, the final result should be an outcome statement (what is going to change), a written action plan (how will we do it), and a progress-monitoring system (how will we keep track of change).

Consulting should *not* be used to remediate the shortcomings of one's colleagues, particularly if these colleagues did not initiate any request for assistance. Consulting should be a structure used by educators who personally choose to increase their effectiveness by seeking information or support from colleagues and/or peers. Upgrading the skills of ineffective teachers is the responsibility of administrators, not peer consultants. To be effective, consulting must occur in an atmosphere of mutual respect where there is no fear of being judged or coerced. For these same reasons, it is difficult for supervisors and administrators who are not usually viewed as peers to serve in the role of consultants to fellow educators. Even though the supervisory process is very similar to the consulting process in its design, the final result of supervision is usually an evaluation of the person's skills—definitely *not* an outcome of consulting.

Consulting is *not* just a structure for identifying and solving problems. It can be used equally well for vision planning. This kind of planning could consist of one person requesting the help of another in designing long-term goals or a desired state of affairs. For example, a teacher may request assistance from a colleague to implement cooperative learning structures or portfolio assessments in his or her classroom. It can also be used for seeking feedback and/or validation for a current state of affairs. In other words, a teacher might request a colleague to evaluate whether he or she is successfully incorporating the essential elements of teacher-directed instruction that are basic to the success of teaching and learning.

WHAT WE WANT WHEN WE CONSULT

When people consult with colleagues, they typically want two things:

1. A substantive outcome.

2. A positive feeling upon completion.

In every relationship and after any encounter, we are likely to want a quality change in addition to leaving with feelings of competence, confidence, and contentment (Fisher & Brown, 1988). To achieve these desired results, it is critical that we use both a planning process and our best communication skills. Substantive outcomes are outcomes that are robust, have long-term value, are generalizable, and address the entire problem. For example, teachers who want students to be more actively involved in their own learning might not want to settle for outcomes that simply result in students raising their hands when they have an answer. This may be only one step on the way to a more substantive outcome such as self-goal setting.

In addition to a substantive outcome, people want positive feelings upon completion. They want to feel good about themselves when the plan is complete. Using effective communications skills such as active listening and open-ended questions are critical to achieving a positive sense of well being. When consulting fails, it is usually because we have forgotten that *people solve problems.* In our haste to get a plan in place, we focus on *solutions* rather than taking sufficient time to listen to the *person* who is experiencing the problem.

When we listen to people, we hear the messages they are sending, not just the words. The *words* state the problem; the *message* contains the whole picture including the feelings behind the problem. Feelings around consulting are often related to fear; either fear of failure or fear of the unknown. The message can only be heard through empathic listening and acceptance of the individual who is likely to be struggling to keep up with today's ever-increasing demands on their time and energy.

An effective way to empathize is to visualize yourself in the consultee's situation as you listen to him or her speak. Try to *feel* what they are telling you. Ask yourself, "What are the feelings buried in these words?" and "What do they really need me to hear?" When you hear the feelings, you hear the *real* message. For example, when a teacher says, "This kid does not belong in my room," what is he or she really saying? The real message may be, "When this student is in my room, I feel helpless and frustrated, and have a sense of personal failure, therefore, he or she must go to another instructional setting so that I can feel better about myself." Or it may be that the teacher does not believe that he or she has the skills and training necessary for providing appropriate instruction for this student. What you hear will determine the path you will take toward the ultimate solution. If you only hear their words, "This kid does not belong in my room," you may find yourself using "brute sanity," that is, believing that you are right and trying to convince a teacher that the student does belong or has a right to be in his or her classroom. If you hear the message, you are more likely to find yourself designing strategies that work for all involved.

If you do *not* hear the message behind what people are saying, the trust necessary for a successful consulting process is in jeopardy. Most people are less concerned about how much their consultants know than how much the consultant cares about them and their problem. This statement is true no matter with whom you are working. For example, we not only want our doctors, lawyers, therapists, or hair stylists to be knowledgeable about their craft, but we also want to believe that they care about our personal well being as they work through our issues with us. We show people we care by listening and valuing what they are saying.

Fisher & Brown (1988) make the importance of listening from the problem initiator's or consultee's point of view crystal clear in the following passage:

> Unless you listen to my views, accept my right to have views
> that differ from yours, and take my interests into account, I
> am unlikely to want to deal with you (p. 12).   C?

Fisher & Brown (1988) also illuminate the importance of effective communication from the facilitator's or consultant's point of view in this passage:

> Unless I have a good idea of what you think the problem
> is, what you want, why you want it, and what you think
> might be fair, I will be groping in the dark for an outcome
> that will meet your interests as well as mine (p. 10). C?

Listening is an important element of many of life's endeavors and essential to successful planning. Because of its importance, two chapters of *Working Together* are dedicated expressly to the skills of communicating. Chapter 4 emphasizes listening skills and Chapter 5 discusses how to express yourself in a way that invites people into the conversation.

WHAT WE DO NOT WANT WHEN WE CONSULT

There are many things that we do not want to experience when we consult with colleagues, several of which have been alluded to in previous sections and will be discussed further in this and remaining chapters. However, there is one major barrier to successful consulting that needs to be made very explicit because it is the one that so many of us create in our innocence and in our kindness. That barrier is: we do not want to consult with people who talk before they listen. We resent people who have quick, easy answers to complex problems even when we seem to directly ask for the help. Having people tell us what to do before we are ready to hear is annoying and an insult to our intelligence. Unfortunately, consultees are not generally trained in the consulting process and as a result, when we are in that role, we do not even know *why* we are not getting what we want or *what* to do about it if we did know. This is true whether we are consulting with colleagues, friends, or spouses. The following short story should illustrate this concept very well.

Reta would often consult with a colleague, Tom, to discuss and solve difficult, work related problems. She typically began the discussion saying, "Tom, I need your help on what to do." Tom, who prided himself as an idea person, was always ready to help. As Reta began painting her picture of the problem, Tom would interrupt and say, "Reta, fortunately it is not that complicated. What you need to do is . . . ," and he would enthusiastically describe what Reta should do.

Each time this occurred (and it occurred every time), Reta became very frustrated and would argue with Tom about how his solutions would not work for her. Tom, whose intentions were only to help, would become perplexed (often hurt) and immediately disengage saying, "I thought you asked for my help!" Reta would now be faced with two problems: the original one still unsolved and her negative feelings about problem solving with Tom. Later, as Reta thought about their problematic discussions, she acknowledged that while Tom did offer valuable solutions, she was unable to listen to or appreciate them. She decided to share her concerns with Tom. Their mutual analysis was revealing. Because Tom was so talented with ideas, his self-esteem increased each time they engaged in problem solving. At the same time, however, Reta's self-esteem plummeted because she began doubting her abilities to solve her problems and, as a result, felt that she was becoming increasingly dependent on Tom. She told Tom that she did not enjoy this feeling at all.

To be more successful problem solvers (and to maintain the relationship), Reta and Tom decided that they needed to examine *the way* in which they worked together. Because Tom's consulting style was unlikely to change—at least not in the near future—they agreed that before Tom would begin telling Reta what to do he would always preface his ideas by saying, "Reta, I have no idea what will work best for you. You are in a much better position to make that decision than I am, but based on the little I know so far about your complex problem, it would seem to me that a couple of ideas you may want to consider are . . . ." With this qualifier, Tom was able to propose many possible solutions and Reta was able to listen to them all. This short phrase allowed Reta to be acknowledged as the real expert on what might work best for her in her situation. As a result, the whole tone of their interactions changed and they were both able to discuss problems and solutions in a more collaborative way.

As you reflect on this short story, you can see the barriers that both Tom and Reta created when they tried to work together. Tom created barriers by jumping in too early to solve Reta's problems; Reta created barriers by not clearly communicating what she really needed from Tom during problem solving. Reta obviously needed to be more explicit about what "help" entailed for her and to stop assuming that Tom understood that what she really wanted him to do was paraphrase, summarize, and clarify the picture she was painting.

Jumping in early with quick, easy answers is not done deliberately to annoy or insult anyone, often it is done innocently by inexperienced consultants and by "seasoned" consultants who believe that they have heard this problem before and want to save time, theirs and their colleagues. But it does not work! Let us review the reasons why:

♦ It is demeaning to someone who is struggling with a problem to have a consultant who is new to the situation provide a quick solution. The unintended message is, "I am so smart and you are so dumb!"

♦ As consultees, we need to feel that our situation is fully understood and our unique situation is acknowledged before we are ready to listen and review intervention options.

♦ All situations are unique. All people are unique. They may seem similar at first, but we must listen for and honor the uniqueness if we want to be heard.

♦ People usually have plenty of answers or solutions at hand; that is not the problem. What people are more likely to need is for a colleague to listen and help them hear the answers they are telling themselves, or lead them to the answers that they perceive themselves capable of implementing. At other times, they may need colleagues to help them acknowledge the problem they are speaking of but have been unable to hear because of the emotions involved. When the problem is identified, the solutions are usually somewhat obvious to the problem initiator.

♦ It is fallacious to believe that we have answers for other people; we only have answers for ourselves. The best we can do is share our ideas so they can be shaped, adapted, altered, or expanded by the problem initiator to fit the situation.

♦ When we provide answers for others, they become dependent on us and may later resent us. Similarly, after the initial glow we get from feeling so smart, we also may resent them for their dependency on us.

It is *not* wrong to offer solutions. People love to entertain ideas. It is our timing and the way we present them that causes colleagues to be resistant and combative at times.

Both the consultant and the consultee have a responsibility to make the process work. Unquestionably, the way we communicate and our timing can either enhance or destroy a sound problem-solving or planning process. In short, it is vital for both parties involved to openly discuss what they need and what they do not need from their colleague. Reading people's minds is very difficult, if not impossible. So, talk to one another about the process. By doing so, you engage in the *art* of consulting.

MODELS FOR CONSULTING

There are many different models, structures, and theories associated with the practice of consulting. They all have distinct as well as common dimensions. The four basic theoretical models applied to educational settings are the behavioral model (Tharp & Wetzel, 1969; Bergen, 1977), the mental health model (Caplan, 1970), the clinical model (Conoley, 1981) and the organizational model (Schein, 1969). A definition of consulting offered by Meyers, Parsons, & Martin (1979), which is a composite from the fields of school psychology, mental health, and organizational development, is as follows:

> [Consulting is] a technique that, at a minimum, always has the following six characteristics: (1) it is a helping, problem-solving process; (2) it occurs between a professional help-giver and a help-seeker who has responsibility for the welfare of another person; (3) it is a voluntary relationship; (4) the help-giver and the help-seeker share in solving the problem; (5) the goal is to help solve a current work problem of the help-seeker; and (6) the help-seeker profits from the relationship in such a way that future problems may be handled more sensitively and skillfully (p. 4). ❀

This definition highlights three important elements: (1) the issue of *personal choice*, (2) the importance of *joint responsibility* when problem solving, and (3) the issue of *empowerment*.

More recent models that have many of the same elements as the basic models are the collaborative model (Idol, Paolucci-Whitcomb, & Nevin, 1986), the instructional model (Alpert & Meyers, 1983), and the peer collaboration model (Pugach & Johnson, 1988a, 1988b, 1988c). The question that begs to be asked is which is the best model to use when consulting with colleagues? The answer is that it depends upon your specific purpose, your preferred style, and the preference of the people with whom you are working. Some people find it useful to use a combination of all these models or to use a different model at different stages of the consulting process. None of these models, including the basic ones mentioned earlier, will be discussed in their pure form in this book, although many of their best elements are discussed throughout the book. If you wish to learn more about each model, consult the original sources listed in the reference section.

LABELS CAN DISABLE THE CONSULTING PROCESS

Do you remember the words of an old country western song that lamented, "We tried to work it out but the words got in the way"? That could not be more true than when we use the words *consultant* and *consultee*. Both words are loaded with meaning and often, among educational practitioners, have a negative connotation. For many, the label consultant conjures up the image of "expert"—one who knows all and tells all and, in some situation, assumes the role of a "hired gun." Unfortunately, for many teachers, a consultant is a person who tells people what to do in their classrooms. In a culture of privatism, this is verboten. For these reasons, many educators are hesitant and uncomfortable about assuming the role of a consultant with their colleagues.

Similarly, for many people the label consultee conjures up an image of someone who is either mildly incompetent and/or dependent—someone who is unable to solve problems unless an expert gets involved and helps them through their sad state of affairs. With these negative images, whether they are held by you or those around you, it takes a great deal of courage to ask for help. In fact, in most schools today, the norm is not to ask for help. The fear is that if you do, what will your colleagues say, and what will the principal think? Going-it-alone has long been the standard practice.

Research suggests that there are psychological benefits and costs associated with the processes of providing and asking for help. As in our short story about Reta and Tom, the consultant's self-esteem was bolstered as he provided help, while the consultee's self-esteem was lowered as she sought relief in the consultant's expertise (Rosenfield, 1987). As you observe some consulting relationships, there is the appearance of a "superior me works with inferior you" attitude. For the consulting process to work, it must be nonhierarchical. While the consultant may have more information or is an expert on a particular subject, that certainly does not qualify him or her as a superior human being.

To take some of the sting out of these words, the labels consultant and consultee will be used interchangeably in this book with less ominous and intimidating terms such as *facilitator* or *peer consultant* and *problem initiator.*

It is important, at this point, not to leave you with a mistaken impression regarding the role of a consultant. A consultant usually has expert knowledge. In fact, the generic definition of a consultant is one who has specialized knowledge, possibly as a result of more or different training and/or experiences. Additionally, if consultees do not believe that consultants can help in some way by means of their insights, ideas, or strategies, they are unlikely to give up their precious time to meet with them. It is the way consultants use or abuse their expertise to set the tone of an interaction that determines its success.

Because most educators are experts in some areas, most educators can be consultants to one another by engaging in cooperative problem solving. In most situations it is possible for the roles of the consultant and consultee to be interchangeable depending on the specific need. Teacher A can consult with Teacher B about a work related problem (e.g., generalizing skills across learning environments) and the next time Teacher B could consult with Teacher A about a plan he or she is developing (e.g., designing building-based teams).

CONSULTING AS A VEHICLE FOR PROFESSIONAL DEVELOPMENT

More and more, schools are making concerted efforts to move away from privatism and individualism where teachers work in isolation toward more collaborative partnerships where *all* professionals create visions together, share expertise and resources, examine existing practices, and engage in reflective inquiry (Fullan & Hargreaves, 1991). Consulting can occur as an integral part of many of these cooperative, professional development activities, or it can be an additional tool for professional interaction (Glatthorn, 1990). For this to happen, the current practice of consulting needs to be reexamined so that all professionals as well as parents can function in the role of the consultant in the problem-solving or planning process. Listed below are the typical practices of consultation in schools today that need to be reexamined because of their limitations in a changing world:

- ◆ People are designated (selected, assigned, appointed, self-appointed) as consultants by virtue of their position. These people tend to be central-office coordinators, content-area specialists (reading, science, computers, etc.), lead teachers, staff developers, special educators, speech/language therapists, teachers of the gifted and talented, Chapter One teachers, English as a Second Language (ESL) teachers, instructional-support teachers (IST), social workers, and school psychologists.

- ◆ Consultees are forced to pick their consultants from a limited pool. They rarely can pick with whom they would like to consult. This practice, alone, inhibits the use of consultants.

- ◆ Consulting is *primarily* something people do when a particular student is in academic or behavioral trouble. It is rarely used as a formal process for professional development such as developing a more efficient classwide, behavior-management system or implementing cooperative-learning structures. (The latter could nullify the former.)

- ◆ Consulting often occurs or is mandated as a preventative measure. This is generally referred to as a prereferral process and occurs before students are placed in special and/or support programs. This process involves either consulting teachers or teacher assistance teams (Chalfant, Pysh, & Moultrie, 1979).

- ◆ Consulting is generally perceived of as an expert-to-novice or top-down relationship with the consultant owning and driving the process.

♦ Consulting is typically problem focused, reactive in nature, and rarely proactive. If no major problems exist, there is no reason to consult.

♦ Consulting occurs between two or more people primarily to help a third party, typically one particular student. This is commonly referred to as a triadic model.

♦ Consultants are expected to have more and different expertise and training than consultees. This often excludes peer teachers who have similar training and expertise.

For consulting to be a school-wide norm that includes all professionals and parents and for it to be an integral part of other professional development activities, conventional thinking and common practices need to change. The new thinking should reflect practices discussed in the following sections.

Consulting can be a reciprocal, mutual activity that occurs among all professionals in the school, including parents

Past practices assumed that only certain people had sufficient expertise to be consultants with their colleagues. Interestingly enough, classroom teachers who are closest to the practice and serve on the front lines every day are generally excluded from this pool of experts. But times are changing. It is becoming increasingly apparent that no one group has a monopoly on truth or knowledge. The future of educational reform depends upon the unleashing of a greatly underutilized resource in our school—classroom teachers (Fullan & Hargreaves, 1991).

Parents, who often spend several hours a day in direct contact with their children, are too often not perceived as consultants to teachers. Parents are a rich source of information for educators, especially parents of students who have moderate to severe learning and emotional problems. These parents have spent hundreds of concentrated hours observing and helping their children learn and develop. Therefore, we have much to learn from them.

Educators who consult in a reciprocal manner (co-consult) experience *mutual* growth. Current research suggests that problem solving and planning with colleagues may be the best form of professional development available to educators. Some educators are experts on designing curriculum outcomes, thinking skills, performance-based assessment, cooperative-learning environments, and thematic units. Others are experts on multiple intelligences, cognitive strategies, learning problems, adaptive strategies, and self-management strategies. No school can afford—financially or intellectually—to waste any of their in-house experts.

When all professionals in the school and parents are trained and feel competent with the skills of consulting, a large pool of consultants is created. This allows consultees the freedom to select with whom they would like to consult on any issue. The practice of forced choice mentioned earlier is a major point of contention in many schools.

Most people are anxious to learn *from* and to learn *with* their colleagues, especially if the school culture values it. People have strong desires to be life-long learners throughout their careers. They believe that people are all either green and growing or ripe and dying! Nobody relishes the feeling of having mentally burned out on the job. Fortunately, when consulting, both the consultant and the consultee can be learners in the process.

Consulting can be a proactive process

Just as the word *night* assumes darkness, the word *consultant* normally assumes a problem. The word *problem* generally implies a weakness, a perplexing condition, a difficulty, or a deficit for which a fix is needed. But just as it is not necessarily dark at night in Alaska, it is not necessary for consulting to occur only in situations where there are problems. Consulting can be a proactive, as well as a reactive, process. For our purposes, a problem is defined as a situation in which a question is proposed for discussion for which a solution is sought because a difference exists between a current state of affairs and a desired future state of affairs.

This definition suggests a broader meaning of the word problem and opens up the doors for consultation to play a role in vision planning and break-the-mold thinking such as redesigning curricular outcomes, changing instructional practices, or designing more authentic assessment practices.

Consulting can play a major role in professional development if it is viewed as a process, not a product, a means, not an end. Success with any one problem or issue is not its endpoint; it is just a step along the road of professional growth. Consulting can foster continuous learning, incessant creativity, and perpetual growth.

Consulting can occur between two or more people and be unrelated to a specific third party

A classic example of a nontriadic model is when you consult with medical doctors. You define the problems you are experiencing then seek their expert advice, and they, in turn, request that you share the responsibility for staying healthy (and sometimes alive) by following through on a mutual decision. During follow-up consultations, modifications are made as you evaluate the results together. There is no third party; it is not a triadic model.

Similarly, consulting can occur between two professionals for the purpose of examining existing curricula or changing one's instructional behavior (Alpert & Meyers, 1983). While it can be argued that it is students who ultimately benefit, consulting was not initiated because of a perceived problem. It is a common and accepted practice in most professions to seek consultation from one's colleagues to learn a new technique. Consultation that is limited to a triadic model generally assumes that the learner is at fault for any learning inadequacies when, in fact, the curriculum, the instructional program or the teacher's instructional style may be the primary cause of a student's failure (Rosenfield, 1987).

Consulting can occur formally or informally among people who have similar, not just different, expertise

As professionals, we regularly approach colleagues who have similar training to gain their insights and ideas. Teachers are more likely to believe the information they hear from colleagues who engage in similar work, than they would believe research findings or information from people whose work is dissimilar to theirs. We have high confidence in people who are just like us. This explains the power and popularity experienced by teacher assistance teams as they were originally designed by Chalfant, Pysh, & Moultrie (1979) where classroom teachers meet regularly to solve student-related problems. (See also *Project RIDE* listed in "For Further Reading.")

When professionals with similar training and expertise consult with colleagues, they generally use a facilitative or a collaborative approach (i.e., there is shared responsibility for problem discovery and problem solution). A peer consultant does not need to feel solely responsible for providing answers to a consultee's questions. The consultant's role is to guide the problem initiator through a problem-solving process and, where appropriate, offer his or her ideas and insights, or any support to which they mutually agree.

It is difficult today to keep up with exponential changes and an ever-increasing diverse population. We cannot win if we continue to conform to past practices or try harder, faster, and longer doing things the same old way. We need all the consultants (in-house experts) we can get to meet the challenges and opportunities of tomorrow, so it is important that everyone feel competent with the skills of problem solving and communicating as they engage in a diverse set of professional interactions with colleagues. The skills discussed in the remainder of this book are generic and therefore applicable to all professional and personal activities.

THE MESSAGE

Life is too short and there are too many resources in our schools to struggle alone. Consulting is one of many structures that educators can use to collaborate with colleagues. It is an effective process for our own professional development and implementing changes in our schools. Consulting is not simply a way to give others advice or a structure we use only when we have problems.

What we want when we consult with colleagues are: (1) substantive outcomes, and (2) positive feelings about ourselves and the experience. What we do not want are answers before questions are fully discussed and understood. To achieve these ends, we need a process for guided discussion and effective communication skills.

2

EFFECTIVE CONSULTING

How do we problem find?
How do we problem solve?

THINKING WELL IS WISE; PLANNING WELL, WISER: DOING WELL, WISEST OF ALL
—*Persian proverb*

We cannot get through a day, either in our professional or personal life, without experiencing problems or pondering how to make our future more successful. Because problem solving and planning are an integral part of our daily routine, it behooves us all to become excellent problem solvers and planners. Having an effective and efficient process for doing so can not only help us achieve the outcomes we want but also help us retain a very precious commodity, our time.

Consulting without a problem-solving process or a planning guide is like a coach sending football players out onto the field without a game plan or a teacher trying to teach a lesson without using an instructional model to guide him or her through the essential elements of lesson design. Can you imagine yourself teaching a lesson on astronomy without first determining what you want students to know (or be able to do), then assessing prior knowledge (what they already know about stars and planets), and finally, finding out if they even have a desire to learn about the celestial dome? The same is true for consulting. An effective problem-solving process serves as a guide through problem discovery to problem resolution. The process moves through a series of steps from what we know now about the problem, what we need to know, how we will solve it, and how we will know when we have solved it. Without a guide we are vulnerable to committing the same sins as the coach or the teacher; we risk brainstorming solutions and making decisions before we have assessed the needs in sufficient detail.

The number of stages in the process can vary depending upon how you choose to design it. Typically, the stages are: (1) entry, (2) problem identification and analysis, (3) planning and decision making, (4) implementation, and (5) follow up and exit. The six major stages of problem solving that will be developed in this chapter are:

1. Start the Conversation

2. Paint the Picture

3. Create a Manageable Scene

4. Design a Feasible Plan

5. Make it Happen

6. Review the Work

These problem-solving stages are more cyclical than linear in nature, as demonstrated in Figure 1.

FIGURE 1

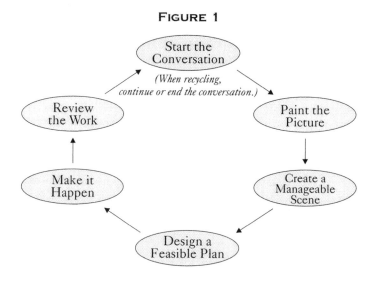

Successful consulting addresses all of these stages in a somewhat orderly fashion. Each of the six stages has a series of specific steps or issues that need to be considered during the process. Each stage is developed in greater detail in this chapter.

The importance of a structured problem-solving process cannot be overstated. Let us review why it is in our best interests to have one:

♦ It serves as a visible road map for both parties to think and plan together.

♦ Without a clear road map, it is easy to get lost on a secondary road or spend time on interesting, but unrelated, issues or the uncontrollable aspects of the problem which we have little to no affect upon, (e.g., alcoholism in the student's family, the disproportionate number of at-risk students in the school or class, lack of sufficient time, etc.).

♦ It makes the process more efficient. Efficiency is important in schools because teachers do not have much school time scheduled for problem solving with colleagues. Collaborative planning time is too often considered a luxury, not a necessity.

♦ It is easy to jump into solution finding before the problem is fully understood or the problem initiator believes it is fully understood.

♦ It helps guarantee that all the stages are addressed so that success is more likely.

GUIDELINES FOR ENSURING SUCCESS

Consulting can, on the surface, appear to be simple and straightforward but, in reality, it is complex and dynamic. There is much to remember as you move through the stages of planning and problem solving. Incorporating the following guidelines are critical to success. As you read each of the following guidelines, reflect on your experiences both as a consultant or a consultee, and try to think of others that need to be added to this list:

♦ *Listening is the heart of problem solving.* Your interpersonal skills determine your personal appeal. The more people like you, the more they will be willing to work with you. You increase your likability factor every time you listen to people and acknowledge their emotional needs. Needs are often a matter of style. (See Chapters 6, 7, and 8 for more information on styles.)

♦ *Jargon interferes with effective listening.* Avoid jargon at all costs because many terms are either unfamiliar or just down-right frightening. They pervade the field: terms like brain-compatible learning, control theory, inclusion, obsessive-compulsive behavior, or acronyms like ADHD, OBE, SST, etc. (You can probably add many more to this list!) Jargon inhibits one's ability to listen to the important information that is being discussed. You are either trying to figure out the meaning from context or wondering if you should feel stupid for not knowing the terms.

♦ *Avoid making yourself feel as helpless as the situation.* Focus your time and efforts on issues that are within your circle of influence (i.e., issues over which you have some control) (Covey, 1992). It is unwise to spend your limited time on causality issues such as inside-the-head factors like memory problems and perceptual disorders, or outside-the-classroom factors like single-family homes and ineffective leadership. These factors are certainly interesting and we should probably be aware of them, but if we focus on them too much, we run the risk of feeling frustrated and discouraged because we literally have no power to influence or change them.

♦ *Honesty and openness increase trust.* As a memory device during problem solving, you may want to jot down comments or questions that you may want to raise later. This practice enables you to listen more effectively. It also allows you to more accurately paraphrase, clarify, reflect, and summarize during the problem-discovery stage. If you do take relevant notes at this time, make sure that you explain what you are doing and why. Also make sure that everyone has access to what you are writing at any time. People need to know that you have no secrets or hidden agendas.

♦ *It amazing how much more sense people make when you really listen to how they view their world.* Avoid judging any comments or suggestions that are made. Try to have an out-of-body experience by making every effort to see either the problem or a possible solution from another's point of view. The way people frame a problem and the solutions they suggest are generally congruent with their beliefs.

♦ *Listen before you talk.* Actively listen to people's beliefs and values. Accept the way they see their world. Remember, you never have to agree. When people feel that their beliefs and values have been acknowledged, they are more likely to allow you to share your beliefs and values. Everyone's views need to be put on the table for discussion, and, where appropriate, challenged before an adequate solution can be devised.

♦ *Consultees also need to use active listening skills.* Consultees must use many of the same skills as their peer consultant if the process is to be successful. They need to paraphrase, clarify, reflect, and summarize their perceptions of what they are hearing and what is occurring.

♦ *Involvement begets acceptance.* The process must meet the needs of the consultee. They are the consumers of the process. People who are actively involved in the problem-solving process should be the same people involved in designing the process that will be used to think, plan, and work together. In those instances where the consultant has received more training in the process, the consultee should at least be aware of the process they will be using when working together *prior* to the actual problem-solving discussion. When the process is complete, it needs to be evaluated in terms of whether it worked effectively or needs to be redesigned for the next time.

◆ *Honor people's emotional needs.* As you listen attentively during the problem-discovery phase, it is important to listen and clarify both the nature of the problem and the person's emotional needs. The problem is usually identified through the verbal content of the discussion; the need is identified primarily through the nonverbal and feeling part of the discussion. If the emotional aspect is ignored, the problem will never be solved. For example, if the problem that is presented is regarding a student who repeatedly lies or cheats and these behaviors are an affront to your values, it is very difficult to discuss possible interventions until your feelings about the behavior are acknowledged.

◆ *Ownership begets commitment.* The more people are involved in the process of planning an intervention, the more ownership they have. The more time and energy people invest in problem solving, the higher the probability of commitment and follow through. People support that which they help create.

STAGES IN THE CONSULTING PROCESS

Stage 1: Start the conversation

A metaphor that can be considered for this element of the problem-solving process is readying a stage for a play. Just as there are many tasks that need to be done in advance if the play is to run smoothly, there are many issues that need to be addressed up-front if the process is to run smoothly. Some of these tasks are as follows:

◆ *Establish rapport.* As you begin the process, it is important to be in harmony with each other, to be in accord, to establish a connection. For this to happen, both verbal and nonverbal communication need to be present. You use verbal communication to design your problem-solving process. You use nonverbal communication to acknowledge emotional needs.

◆ *Discuss your philosophy.* We each hold certain beliefs about teaching and learning. Honor and celebrate differences when they occur. There is no doubt that we get more comfort and assurance from people whose philosophy is similar to ours, but we are likely to learn more from people who think differently.

◆ *Discuss the purpose of the meeting.* In other words, why are we meeting? What is the nature of the problem? At this point, it is simply an overview statement like, "I want to learn more about cooperative learning structures," or "I need information on how to include a student with severe language problems during group discussion." A full-blown description and analysis occurs in the next stage.

◆ *Set expectations.* These questions need to be addressed: How long are we meeting? What happens if we do not accomplish our mutual agenda within the timelines we set? What is discussed outside this room? What is not (the confidentiality issue)? Is there joint responsibility for the outcomes? What needs to happen for us not to feel our time has been wasted? Do we have the capacity to solve this problem? Is the problem within our circle of influence? Should anyone else be involved?

◆ *Discuss and outline a problem-solving process.* It is important that you discuss the process you will use as you think and plan together. Either design one or borrow one, but have one!

◆ *Clarify roles.* The key question is: How will we work together to accomplish our goal? Does the consultee want the consultant's role to be facilitative, collaborative or authoritative in nature? (See Chapter 3, Interactive Consulting.)

Stage 2: Paint the picture

On the surface this stage appears to be the simplest, but it is one of the most difficult. In part, the challenge is to define the problem so clearly that the best solutions are uncovered. A major part of problem discovery is asking the right questions because we know that solutions are obvious once you get the questions right (Sculley, 1989). It is the responsibility of the problem initiator to paint a picture of the problem as clearly as he or she can. It is the responsibility of the facilitator to make sure that he or she get as clear a picture as possible by asking questions when the picture is not clear and intermittently describing the picture that they are seeing to verify their own understanding.

Too often, we race through this stage. It is likely that at least 50% of the time that is available should be allocated for this stage alone. A good way to monitor this is to set a timer in advance and not move to the next stage even when you think you understand the problem. The major tasks that need to be accomplished in stage two are as follows:

♦ *Establish a goal statement.* A good way to do this is to think about it this way: When the problem is solved, what does it look like, or when will the problem no longer be a problem? Some examples are: Will the students in question be reading 120 words per minute with less than seven errors in any fourth-grade book? Will you be able to use peer-mediated structures? Will you be able to teach students cognitive strategies? Will a student with attention problems be able to actively participate during all phases of a lesson?

It is important that the goal not be stated in a way that suggests or implies a solution. For example, stating that you would like all the students to be fluent with phonics suggests that the solution for increasing reading skills is to teach phonics. Similarly, to state that you would like to teach organizational or memory strategies suggests that these are the strategies students need. Finally, to state that the student with attentional problems should remain on-task and in his or her seat for a 40-minute period suggests that the task the student is being asked to do does not need to be examined for its relevance and meaning. If too many goals are stated, prioritize and select which one you will focus on first.

Before proceeding to the next step, check for mutual understanding of the goal by restating it and asking for confirmation.

◆ *Describe and analyze the problem.* Describe how things are now and what is causing the stress or concern. A good way to get a clear description of the problem is to ask questions or make statements similar to the following:

- Paint a word picture of the problem as you see it.
- If I (we) were in your situation, what would I (we) be seeing and feeling?
- If someone walked into your class on a bad day, what might they see?

Problems need to be described in specific, behavioral terms, not in vague generalities like, "Students have low self-esteem and are unmotivated to achieve." While this may appear to be true, it is difficult to get a clear picture of exactly what behaviors support these conclusions. The description should focus on behaviors that we can see, hear, touch, smell, and taste. Clarity would increase significantly if we were to describe the problem with statements like these: Students do not complete assigned work; they skip classes; they do not actively participate during teacher-directed instruction or guided practice activities; they do not volunteer comments or ask questions; and they make negative comments about themselves such as, "I am dumb" during student-teacher interviews.

The next step is to analyze the information and try to make sense of it by looking for patterns and connections. Various dimensions of the problem such as, where does it occur, when does it happen, how long does it last, how often does it happen, and at what intensity, are put under a microscope so that later a determination can be made about the best road to take to get from where we are now to where we want to be—our goal. Opposing points of view need to be encouraged when framing the problem. Whenever possible, secure information from a number of sources regarding how the student behaves in other settings. Where necessary, identify any new information that needs to be made available for future discussion, such as how much homework is the student required to complete each night? Does he or she skip other classes? And so on.

♦ *Discuss prior interventions.* Discuss any strategies that have been implemented to date and what the results of those efforts have been. Analyze why (under what conditions) some strategies worked, even if only for a short period of time, and why some strategies did not work or worked only partially. Investigate how changes were monitored. Did the monitoring system address the concern? Over what period of time were the changes implemented? What concrete data were collected that can be analyzed; for example, learning logs, written language samples, behavioral counts, anecdotal records, portfolios, videos, etc.

♦ *Identify the positives.* If the problem is a student, discuss his or her strengths. This information is essential because any future intervention plan is likely to be designed around the student's strengths, not the deficits. Strengths can and should include these areas:

- Present level of performance in academic skill areas.
- Physical and emotional strengths.
- Cognitive abilities (concepts, creativity, language facilities, artistic abilities, intuitiveness, spatial awareness).
- Interpersonal skills with peers and adults.
- Motivational state.
- Intrapersonal intelligence.
- Family support.

If the problem is about implementing or altering a program, many of the same types of questions apply. Discuss the strengths of the situation or the strengths of the implementor. In other words, what is in place, or what do we have going for us?

♦ *Identify the barriers.* What are the elements that you cannot count on? What do you need to circumvent if possible? Physical disabilities like blindness or deafness are certainly an important variable to consider in addition to emotional problems. When dealing with emotional problems, a student might be unable to self-monitor his or her own program.

Stage 3: Create a manageable scene

During this stage, narrow the focus. Revisit your goal and decide what you would like to see happen first and in the next three weeks. What needs to happen for you to experience some early success? Some guidelines for narrowing the focus are:

♦ *Do a task analysis.* A good way to do this is break the goal down into learner objectives. For example, if your goal was that all students in your class will read 120 words per minute with less than seven errors in any fourth-grade book, then your initial objective might be that all students will increase a minimum of ten words per minute from where they are now. If your goal was that you will be able to use peer-mediated instructional strategies in your classroom, then your initial objective might be that you will implement the structure, Heads Together (Kagan, 1990) during the guided practice part of a science lesson.

♦ *Write a specific, observable (measurable) objective.* We are all familiar with the statement, "If you do not know where you are going, then you have no way of determining when you have arrived." It could not be more applicable than in this stage of problem solving. The reading objective stated earlier is specific and can even be charted by the students themselves because it is so clear. The second objective would also be very easy to measure as it is stated, but it may have an inherent weakness in that it is not tied to outcomes. In other words, if you did manage to implement peer-mediated instruction, what would you hope to achieve? Would the students increase their response accuracy? Would students who generally do not participate become more active and engage in more social interactions? Although it could be argued that when teachers use effective practices, student achievement increases, it is always best to track these changes in student behavior.

When problem solving fails, it is generally because we are too vague when writing the objectives and, as a result, too vague about what will change following an intervention. The following objectives exemplify the point; because they are not measurable, it is impossible to track any changes:

- Martha will behave in school.
- George will be more motivated.
- Henrietta will improve her visual memory skills.
- Steve will have higher self-esteem.

If you design an intervention around these vague outcomes, how will you know if it is working? How will you know when Martha is behaving? What will she be doing? What will George *do* when he is motivated? Clear, concrete objectives must lend themselves to performance-based measures. The following examples are more measurable and, as a result, lend themselves to keeping track of any changes in behavior:

- Martha will raise her hand and ask permission to speak during teacher-directed instruction.
- George will complete assignments at 80% accuracy and within the timelines that are mutually negotiated.
- Henrietta will correctly spell ten nonphonetic words from her weekly reading assignments.
- Steve will accept and make positive self-affirmation following the completion of an important and difficult task.

When you have defined precisely what you want and for what purpose, you have probably written an objective that is clear to students, parents, and you.

♦ *Make the objective realistic and attainable.* We all want success, we thrive on it! So be kind to yourself (and your students) by setting yourself up for early success. You may decide to work on your objective only during a certain period, but not the entire day. Also, be careful not to write too many objectives for the same time period.

An excellent strategy to help the problem initiator set an objective that makes sense is to ask questions similar to the following:

- "Given that your goal will take some time to accomplish, where would you like to begin?"
- "If you were to feel successful in three weeks from now, what one thing would you like to see change?"
- "What part of this problem gives you the most stress?"

♦ *Focus on the positive.* Whenever possible, write an objective that communicates growth rather than trying to eliminate an inappropriate behavior. For example, focus on and monitor on-task, in-seat behavior rather than off-task, out-of-seat behavior. Focus on what students now remember as a result of your efforts teaching memory strategies rather than all the things they forgot. You win get more power out of catching yourself or your students being good than the opposite. (Besides, it is less depressing to focus on the positive!)

♦ *Set timelines.* The questions to address are: How long do you anticipate it will take to accomplish the objective that you set? If you do or do not accomplish it in this time period, what needs to happen so that progress can continue?

Stage 4: Design a feasible plan

Once you have decided where you are going, you can decide *how* to get there. For a plan to be feasible, it must stay within our knowledge base and resources should be available to implement it. For example, we might want to suggest that students be given "smart pills" to increase their learning rate. While that might be very desirable, we do not as yet have the knowledge base to do this. Similarly, we may want to suggest that we be provided an "extra set of hands" to implement a program, but it may be that that option is outside our circle of control, albeit within our circle of influence (Covey, 1989).

But neither do we want to be limited to believing that we can only have what is known to be possible. We often create limits for ourselves by only asking for what we think we can get or believe we can do. A more productive approach might be to assume (for a fanciful moment) that you are living in a perfect world and you can have or do anything you want. What, then, would you ask for or do? Could you get an "extra set of hands" from the community, from another class via cross-age tutoring, or by using cooperative-learning groups? When and wherever possible, try to push the boundaries. Stretch beyond your personal horizons and help others reach their outer limits. Doing this might help achieve a near perfect solution.

Some important tasks and considerations that need to be addressed during this stage for the process to be successful are as follows:

♦ *Explore the options.* Everyone needs to participate in this process especially the problem initiator. If he or she is not involved, there is little ownership of the problem and its solution. Without ownership, there is little commitment to implementing the plan with integrity—a frustrating experience for everyone!

It is often good practice to begin the process by asking consultees the following questions to start their thinking (and yours):

  - "What are your thoughts on how this problem might be solved?"
  - "What kinds of strategies have you used in the past for similar problems?"
  - "Have you ever awakened at three o'clock in the morning and asked yourself, 'What if I . . . and what does that look like?'"

Because consultees are closest to the problem, they often have a pretty good handle on what a feasible and manageable solution looks like. Frequently, consultees have the answer but are seeking affirmation or support from their colleagues. Encouraging consultees to think out loud allows others a chance to tap into their current thinking and frame of reference. Once that has happened, a process called *chaining* can occur, that is, one idea triggers a similar idea that has a high probability of working.

It is possible that the strategies mentioned above may be unnecessary on some occasions. Frequently, as the problem is being clarified through analysis and debate, the best solution becomes obvious to the problem initiator. As he or she reflects on his or her practice, it occurs to him or her what needs to happen in order to feel successful in this situation. The discussion then shifts to the next step in this stage.

When more than two people are involved in creating options, excellent strategies such as brainstorming, brainwriting, and nominal group technique are used to encourage divergent thinking and develop a wide range of possible solutions from which to select. The group brain, or in some instances, the dual brain is a truly amazing process in terms of what possibilities can be created. Two heads are always better than one.

In those rare instances where consultees expect consultants to provide all the options, or when consultants are unable to participate in the process because they lack sufficient information on the topic, consultants must be extremely cautious how they present their ideas. The following statements may protect consultants from being solely responsible for the success or failure of the strategies they might have suggested:

- "I can provide some options for you to consider, but you are in the best position to know which ones best fit your teaching style, this student, and your unique situation."

- "Let me share how I have seen others handle a similar situation, then we need to discuss how to adapt it to your situation."
- "I am not sure how we eventually are going to solve this problem. Let me think out loud and you pick out the ideas that make sense to you."
- "I have some ideas but we really need to work together to determine what fits best for you."
- "I am wondering what would happen if . . . ."

After options have been presented, consultees need to be actively involved in adapting strategies to their unique situation if they are to feel responsible and have ownership of their successes.

On occasion, no intervention plan is discussed, but an assessment plan is designed. New ways to collect more information about the problem are outlined. This often happens when it becomes apparent that there is insufficient data to make a responsible decision about an intervention. The discussion then shifts to what information is needed and how it will be collected. For example, what may initially appear to be a reading problem may, in fact, be more related to spoken language. Assessment now focuses in this area.

♦ *Make a decision.* Problem initiators play a primary role in making the final decision. This makes a good sense since they ultimately are the ones who will implement it. Any plan must make sense to them, they must feel comfortable with it, it must fit with their beliefs and values, as well as their teaching styles. The question that needs to be asked is, "Can I really see myself doing this effectively and with integrity?"

There may be times when a rating scale is used to judge the pros and cons of each proposed option. This process illuminates the best solution for solving the problem. Questions that need to be addressed at this point are:

- Do the proposed options relate to the goal?
- Do the options satisfy the goal and how?

- Are the options clear and feasible?
- What resources are needed, if any?
- Are the required resources (time, staff, materials) available?
- Can the change be managed?
- Can the options be sustained over time?
- Are the options adaptable?

◆ *Outline the tasks.* After selecting the best option, an intervention plan needs to be clearly delineated in an orderly fashion. The first step of the plan should be made very clear because this is where most plans fall apart. When the person responsible for carrying out the plan is not sure how to get started, everything can stop until help arrives. Following this, each succeeding step is then fleshed out.

Before proceeding, roles and responsibilities may need to be clarified if more than one person is involved in implementing the plan.

◆ *Write the plan.* Never leave a meeting without a plan in writing. If time runs out, find ten minutes later in the day to get this useful information in writing. It is in everyone's best interest to do so. If it is not written down, it is too easy to forget it or leave out some important steps and, as a result, another great idea slips away unused. Furthermore, it should not be left up to the consultees to figure out at a later time what they envisioned themselves doing. Nor should it be left up to the consultants to write the plan at a later time when no one else is present. When this happens, consultants run the risk, unknowingly, of writing the plan they would like to see implemented, not necessarily the plan that was discussed. Again, ownership is at risk.

A good practice is for the consultant to be the recorder while the consultee describes (or dictates) the plan that they see themselves implementing. There are several advantages for doing it this way. As the consultee visualizes each step in the plan, he or she is really getting their first practice. It is a lot easier to implement it the second time around in the class-room. Also, because consulting is similar to a pull-out pro-gram, it suffers the same downsides, that is, it is difficult to generalize a plan from the meeting room to the classroom. Describing the plan as you visualize it helps with the gener-alization process.

When the steps have been outlined, and if it seems appro-priate, assign time lines for each step in the plan. Timelines are just good practice; they keep us focused and on-task.

♦ *Design a plan for monitoring change.* No plan is complete until the criteria for success have been spelled out. The question that is addressed here is: How will we know if we accom-plished what we set out to achieve? The primary reason for making the goals and objectives explicit and measurable initially was to make change easy to track later. Both teachers and students can monitor these changes and actually see their own growth toward the goal. There is nothing more motivating to students than to have the power and responsi-bility for monitor and chart their own growth. It is equally motivating for teachers to see changes in student behavior that are a direct result of their efforts.

When changes are monitored with an appropriate measuring tool on a regular basis, opportunities are clear and abundant for making early alterations to a plan. Like losing weight, if you do not have a good system for regular monitoring, you may not be diligent in executing your plan. You may get discouraged and quit if you have expended tremendous efforts over a long period of time but did not check in until it was too late to make necessary adjustments along the way.

Qualitative and quantitative performance-based measures like curriculum-based assessments, portfolios, actual work samples, projects, behavioral counts, and interviews are all strategies for monitoring change. Whenever appropriate, use graphs or charts to make clear visual displays of growth.

♦ *Finalize the plan.* Before you can make it happen, a few details need to be addressed. These typically include: (1) review and refine the plan where needed, (2) check for agreement, and (3) set a follow-up date. The question is: where and when will you meet again to review progress toward the goal? The important thing to remember is: Always follow up! Too often, well intentioned plans for follow up are abandoned for any number of good reasons. Lack of time is the most common cause. Too much is at stake to not follow up. Following up prevents people from feeling abandoned, alone in the struggle, dumped on, or viewing an ineffective plan as a personal failure.

It might be wise at this point in the process to remind ourselves that very few plans work perfectly the first time. It is similar to skiing foreign terrain. Many of us have never been on this mountain top before, so we are not exactly sure what to expect until we put our equipment on and start down. As we get new information, we can make the adjustments that may be required to get to the bottom without too many injuries. Because of a wide range of individual differences and circumstances, plans must constantly be adapted and altered to find the best fit for the teacher or the student and the environment. The purpose of follow up is to discuss any necessary adjustments.

♦ *Reflect on the process.* To this point, all our energies have been focused on the problem and its solution. Because the process (i.e., the way we work together) plays a major role in our success, it is always good practice to take a few minutes and debrief the process collaboratively. Some of the questions that might be posed for discussion are as follows:

- "How did our problem-solving structure work for us?"
- "What parts of the overall process did we value and why?"
- "What parts of the process need to be changed and why?"
- "What new insights did we gain?"
- "What should we celebrate?"
- "What are our feelings about the process in general?"

People who use this process frequently develop a debriefing form that they use at the end of every meeting. Like any good partnership that lasts over time, as much attention should be paid to the *way* we do things (our process) as to *what* we get done (our product).

Stage 5: Make it happen

It is now time to execute the plan, to do what we said we would do. During the interim—following designing the plan (stage 4) and before reviewing the plan (stage 6)—some things to consider to assure success are:

♦ *Provide support to one another.* It is especially important during the initial stages of implementing a plan when the risk of failure is highest to be readily available for assistance. Support can take many forms. They typically include (1) ongoing informal contacts, in person or by telephone, (2) peer coaching, to provide structured feedback, and (3) modeling a strategy with follow-up discussion.

♦ *Implement the plan with integrity.* It is very easy to be excited about a plan when leaving a meeting, but to fail to implement it the way it was initially designed. This can happen for three reasons: (1) the plan is not as clear as we initially believed, (2) to our amazement, the problem or the need miraculously disappeared, (3) things changed when we returned to the classroom, and (4) what we thought was the problem is not really the problem. Often we do not know this until we try to implement the plan. The implementation itself provides new information and insights.

Barring these three possibilities, we should try to stick as closely to the original plan as possible for two reasons. The first is obvious: we need to determine if the strategy we designed will work in this situation. The second is a little less obvious. Frequently when we implement a new strategy, we will experience what has been referred to as an implementation dip (Fullan, 1991), that is, things often get worse before they get better. (Do you relate to the phenomenon?)

As you might guess, if we do not commit to sticking with a plan as it was designed for a period of time, past the implementation dip, we can easily become discouraged and quit. We believe at this point that the plan is not working for any number of reasons: It is too intrusive; it is the wrong strategy; or it is a good plan in the wrong situation.

Stage 6: Review the work

Since we have invested so much time and energy in planning and implementation, it is equally important that we now review our work and make some new decisions. They typically are the following:

◆ *Evaluate the plan.* One of the major tasks when following up is to collaboratively evaluate the progress made toward the goal. We now review our goals and objectives and, using our assessments tools, we determine if we achieved what we set out to achieve. The questions we address are:

- "Where was progress made?"
- "Where was progress not made?"
- "Why was progress not made?"
- "What part of the plan worked?"
- "What part failed and why?"
- "Was the plan implemented with integrity?"
- "What part of the plan had to be altered, if any?"
- "How was the plan altered and why?"
- "What new information did we acquire?"
- "What new information do we need?"

◆ *Celebrate.* If you got what you wanted, celebrate! If you did not get what you wanted, celebrate anyway! Celebrate your partnership. Celebrate your investment of time and energy to a worthwhile cause. Celebrate your new learning. You cannot try something new without learning something new. You may have learned how difficult and complex new strategies are to implement. You may have learned how difficult and complex the problem-solving process is. You may have learned what a risk-taker you are. Or you may have learned what you never want to do again!

What you should never do is spend any time establishing guilt, fault, or blame if the plan did not work the way you had hoped. Not only would this action be a fruitless endeavor, but it would obviously damage the relationship that you have probably worked hard to establish.

◆ *Determine future needs.* After successes and problem areas have been analyzed, future needs should be discussed. The question that is addressed is: Should the process be continued or discontinued? If the goals have been achieved and there are no new areas to develop, the process stops here. If the goals have been achieved and there are new areas to develop, the process continues and three things can happen: (1) new goals and objectives are developed, (2) the existing plan is extended, and/or (3) the existing plan is generalized to other settings. If the goals have *not* been achieved, the discussion centers around strategies for fine-tuning the original plan or changing the plan. Follow-up meetings usually continue until the goals have been achieved or until all parties agree to discontinue the process.

◆ *Reflect on the process.* Again, take time to reflect on the process: your planning guide (Did it work for you?); the time and energy you expended (Was it worth it?); the relationships that you developed (Are they valuable?). Many of the questions that were raised at the end of stage 4 can be revisited here. Essentially, you are asking what would you keep and what would you change.

A PROBLEM-SOLVING WORKSHEET

A problem-solving worksheet that is closely aligned to your problem-solving structure should be used as a guide during a problem-solving session. The worksheet serves these five purposes:

1. It helps you remember the stages and steps within each stage.

2. It allows you to take notes during problem discovery, as well as when you are exploring options for solving the problem.

3. It communicates that consulting is not an aimless discussion with no resulting action plan.

4. You have a written plan to refer to when the process is complete.

5. It guarantees that all the stages are addressed so that the best solutions are determined.

There are many different problem-solving models and many different ways to organize problem-solving worksheets around these models (Phillips & McCullough, 1992). If you are new to the practice of consulting, you may want to begin with an established or well-researched process. Just as an artist needs to learn the basic rules of painting before he or she adds her or his own technique, you may need to learn the basic rules of problem solving before creating your own model or designing worksheets to meet your unique needs.

A problem-solving worksheet that has been used extensively over the past ten years by many consultants and consultees is shown in Figure 2. Extensive research supports its efficacy. However, it is unlikely that problem solving in real life situations is carried out in such a tightly structured format because, by nature, it is an active, dynamic process. However, every effort should be made to address each area in an orderly fashion. A follow-up log, that has also been used extensively by the author when problem solving with teachers, is shown in Figure 3.

To increase the worksheet's efficacy, the process needs to be continuously evaluated and redesigned, if necessary, by the people who are involved in the actual processes of thinking, planning, and working together.

FIGURE 2

Problem-Solving Worksheet (page 1)

Descriptive Information _____

Teacher(s) _____

Date _____Student/Class_____

Problem/Issue/Vision: (Why are we meeting?)

1. _____

2. _____

3. _____

Problem Analysis: (What questions need to be addressed? What data need to be examined? How do we make sense of the information available to us?)

Results of Prior Interventions: (What has been tried and how well did it work?)

Student/Situation Strengths: (What is already at mastery or in place?)

Desired Outcome: (What is our overall goal and what is our initial focus?)

Problem-Solving Worksheet (page 2)

Possible Solutions:
(What are the options?)

Rating:			
1.	Great	Possible	Not now
2.	Great	Possible	Not now
3.	Great	Possible	Not now
4.	Great	Possible	Not now
5.	Great	Possible	Not now

Preferred Solution: (Which one seems best for me?)

Implementation Plan: (Exactly how do I/we do this?)   When:

Monitoring Plan: (How do I/we keep track of change?)

Follow-Up Plan: (When do we assess actual changes?)

FIGURE 3

Follow-Up Log

Descriptive Information _____

Teacher(s) _____

Date _____Student/Class_____

Desired Outcome: (What was our overall goal and our initial focus?)

Results of Implementation Plan: (What evidence do we have about what worked?)

Next Step:

      _____ problem solved—case closed

      _____ problem solved—new problem to consider

      _____ problem not solved—revisions needed

      _____ problem not solved—other resources needed

Revisions Needed:

THE MESSAGE

Problems and opportunities are a part of the fabric of life. Therefore, we all need to be skilled and confident in approaching problems, making decisions, and evaluating our efforts. Effective problem solving/consulting means that we use a structured process to guide our thinking from problem discovery to problem resolution. Each stage in a problem-solving process has several steps that need to be addressed if we are to experience the results we want. This chapter walked you through each of them and provided you with ways to put your thoughts into words.

3

TO LISTEN WELL IS AS POWERFUL A MEANS OF COMMUNICATION AND INFLUENCE AS TO TALK WELL.
—*Chief Justice John Marshall (1801-1835)*

How can I interact with them?
How can they interact with me?

hink of a time recently when you consulted with someone or someone consulted with you. As you reflect on this experience, how did you consult with him or her? For the most part, did you listen as he or she thought aloud about the problem? Did you choose to think with him or her about options he or she could consider? Or did you feel it was important to give some critical information that he or she could use to solve a problem? Interactive approaches when consulting are similar to the different ways you might have a conversation with a friend. There are times you lead (do most of the talking), there are times you follow (listen), and there are times you share reciprocally (both listen and talk). The circumstances and the person dictate the interactive approach you use.

There are basically three different interactive approaches you can use when you consult with colleagues. They are commonly referred to as:

1. The Facilitative Approach

2. The Collaborative Approach

3. The Authoritative Approach

It takes a special kind of expertise to use any one of these approaches. All three approaches need *process* expertise, but some need more *content* expertise. While each approach has unique characteristics that distinguish it from the others, there is a great deal of commonalty across the categories.

Some approaches are definitely more appropriate in some situations so it is important to know the critical behaviors of each, as well as when each is *most* appropriate. For example, you may pride yourself as a great facilitative listener and prefer that approach when working with colleagues, but if a colleague approaches you in an apparent high state of anxiety and asks you to tell him or her what to do because he or she has a student in class who is wielding a knife, it is probably inappropriate to respond with a pensive, reflective statement such as, "So you are feeling a lot of fear right now . . . ." He or she needs an answer *now*! The processing of the experience can come later when the crisis has passed. However, if a colleague approaches you to determine the best way to teach reading to an at-risk student that he or she has in class, you are more likely to use active listening and mutual problem solving. But if a colleague who is knowledgeable about different instructional practices in reading wants to reflect on the effectiveness of what he or she is doing, you are likely to engage primarily in facilitative listening. An in depth look at each of these interactive approaches is valuable.

THE FACILITATIVE APPROACH

Let us begin by asking: What are the key behaviors of a facilitative approach and what are the primary tools of a consultant using this approach? When consultants use a facilitative approach, they, in essence, function like a guide-on-the-side, a coach—one who attempts to guide the problem initiator using the process of reflective thinking. The consultant helps a colleague search through the relevant data that the consultee has collected in order to find his or her own solutions. Consultants work hard to keep the problem initiator on stage through the entire problem finding and planning process. They do *not* put themselves on stage with the consultee either by taking control of the questions that need to be addressed or offering possible solutions that could be implemented. Because the problem initiator is believed to be an expert on the problems he or she faces and their ultimate solutions, the primary role of the consultant is to guide the problem initiator through a problem-solving and planning format and ensure that each step in the process is addressed.

Facilitative consulting is a very metacognitive process in that it allows consultees to think about their own thinking, to ponder, and to reflect on a problem in such a way that appropriate solutions seem more evident to them. Throughout this process the consultant has trust in people's "capabilities to own their own problems while also respecting their existing levels of expertise as problem solvers" (Pugach & Johnson, 1988a, p. 5). The primary tools of this approach are active listening, paraphrasing, clarifying questions, summarizing, predicting, and self-questioning. A typical question that a consultant might ask a consultee who has indicated that he or she has a problem with a student who never completes his work is, "When you reflect on this problem, what questions do you ask yourself about this student not completing his work?" The consultee might then ask himself or herself a series of questions, such as the following:

♦ What strategies have I used to assure that the student has acquired the concepts or skills to complete the work successfully?

♦ Have I made it clear why it is important to complete the assigned tasks?

♦ What is the nature of the work the student does complete or at least start?

♦ Does the student understand the consequences of not completing work?

♦ Should I interview the student privately to discuss what interferes with him completing work?

Following problem discovery, the consultant encourages the problem initiator to think of possible solutions and make predictions about how these solutions might solve the problem (Pugach & Johnson, 1988a). This approach assumes that the problem initiator knows most of the critical questions that need to be addressed and, as a result, possesses the solutions. It promotes and supports independent problem solving and, as a result, self-sufficiency (Pugach & Johnson, 1988a). It adheres to the belief that solutions are obvious once you get the questions right (Sculley, 1987).

The facilitative approach is most appropriate when: (1) the consultee is a peer who has similar training and expertise as the consultant, (2) it is obvious that the consultee has adequate knowledge or experience with the subject at hand, and (3) the consultee openly requests this approach.

The strengths of the facilitative approach is its total respect for the competence of one's colleagues, and that it gives true meaning to the word *empowerment*.

THE COLLABORATIVE APPROACH

What are the key features of a collaborative approach and what are the primary tools of a consultant using this approach? When consultants use a collaborative approach, they function as a co-equal member of a pair (or a team). They work as partners side-by-side as they investigate and solve a problem. They search through relevant data with the problem initiator in order to find solutions that are satisfactory to both of them. They share the stage with the problem initiator during the problem-solving and planning process. They freely offer new or different perspectives on an issue or problem. There is a shared responsibility for raising critical questions, collecting data, proposing solutions, and determining strategies for keeping track of changes.

The collaborative approach uses many of the same skills as the facilitative approach: active listening, clarifying questions, summarizing, predicting, and self-questioning. It also uses leading questions (questions that lead the consultee to new and or different insights or perspectives), mutual idea generating, and brainstorming. A collaborative consultant might make this comment to the teacher mentioned earlier who was concerned about the student who never completed work, "What questions do we need to ask ourselves about this student not completing his work?" Other questions and comments a collaborative consultant might ask are:

- ◆ "Shall we investigate whether the student has the concepts or skills to complete work?"

- ◆ "How can we determine if the student sees the relevance of completing this task?"

- ◆ "What is the nature of the work the student does complete? What can that tell us?"

- ◆ "Let us look at what happens when the student does not complete work."

- ◆ "I wonder if it would be valuable for you to meet with the student privately to discuss why he is not completing work?"

As you can see from these questions, the consultant plays a more active role in this approach than in the facilitative approach. Friend & Cook (1992) offer some defining characteristics of collaboration that have implications for collaborative consulting. They are:

- ◆ *Collaboration is based on mutual goals.* People must have a commitment to the goals on which they are currently working. For example, both people in a collaborative approach commit to the goal of increasing reading skills for a student or all students in a class, but their methods may differ. One person may believe in a whole language approach, the other, a phonetic approach, but both agree to focus on the goal of increasing reading skills before discussing the how.

- ◆ *Collaboration requires parity among participants.* People's contributions must be equally valued and they must have equal decision making power in the activity in which they are currently involved. Whether they advocate the whole-language approach or the phonetic approach, both teachers listen to, value, and respect each other's research and personal experiences regarding the two different reading programs. They do not dismiss each other's information out-of-hand because it does not fit with his or her previous beliefs or experiences.

If one person has, or is perceived to have, more valuable knowledge or greater decision making power, the process cannot be described as collaborative. In other words, if one person continuously defers to the other because one has more extensive training and, as a result, more valuable information in reading instruction, or if one person alone makes the final decision about which strategy to implement, it is not a collaborative approach. For the process to be collaborative, both teachers need to achieve consensus. They might decide, for example, to monitor reading performance over a four to six week period of time, first, using a phonetic approach, then a more holistic approach for another four to six weeks. The effectiveness of each is then evaluated through performance assessments or curriculum-based measurements.

♦ *Collaboration depends on shared responsibility for participation and decision making.* Both people are actively involved in designing and determining an appropriate intervention, but how they share the responsibility for implementing the plan does not necessarily mean that they have to divide the tasks equally or to fully participate in every task. It is more often a division of labor based on available time, roles and responsibilities, and individual skills.

Continuing with the reading skills example, several options are possible: (1) Both people may work together to design reading strategies but only one actually implements them; (2) One person chooses to be responsible for all the reading instruction while the other chooses to either be responsible for monitoring reading progress weekly or teaching students how to graph their own results; and (3) One person may be responsible for all the reading instruction and assessment while the other only reflects on the data with his or her colleague, after which they mutually discuss possible alternatives if the results are unsatisfactory.

♦ *Collaboration requires shared responsibility for outcomes.* People share responsibility for both the success or failure of a mutually agreed upon endeavor. If it was decided that a phonetic approach would be implemented for six weeks, then both stand accountable for the results—good or bad. In other words, one party does not stand by feeling smug and assume an "I told you so" attitude if the results of the intervention favor his or her preferred instructional strategy.

♦ *Collaboration requires that participants share their resources.* People must be willing to share information, access to information, materials, equipment, and, yes, even instructional aides if they are available.

♦ *Collaboration is a voluntary relationship.* People cannot be coerced or mandated to collaborate. If and when they are, it is an oxymoron. Fullan & Hargreaves (1991) refer to forced collaboration as "contrived collegiality (p. 58)." They do suggest, however, that directives or district policies encouraging collaboration may be a necessary first step.

Consulting is a collaborative effort when all six elements are applied to the problem-solving or planning process. The theme of this approach is that two heads are better than one and we sink or swim together as is the case with cooperative learning (Johnson, Johnson, Holubec, & Roy, 1984).

The collaborative approach is most appropriate when the consultant and consultee: (1) share responsibility for the same students as is the case with general educators and special services; (2) have a vested interest in the success of a program or a group of students (mutual goals); (3) share accountability for outcomes of a program; and (4) want to develop a collaborative ethic in their school that advocates that all students are the responsibility of all teachers.

The collaborative approach works best when there is an atmosphere of trust among colleagues, a mutual respect for other people's interpersonal and teaching styles, and everyone feels comfortable with the skills for achieving consensus.

The strengths of the collaborative approach are that educators do not feel alone in the struggle to meet the needs of all students, there is a support system in place for all teachers, and it also increases mutual respect and trust among colleagues.

THE AUTHORITATIVE APPROACH

What are the key features of an authoritative approach and what are the primary tools of a consultant using this approach? When consultants use an authoritative approach, they assume more of an expert role, a sage-on-the-stage who takes primary responsibility for determining the critical questions, collecting relevant data (or overseeing the data to be collected), providing solutions, and evaluating the results. Because they have special knowledge and experiences related to the issue or subject under discussion, they function as information experts; like conductors, they direct the symphony; they make suggestions; they give advice; they oversee the process.

The authoritative approach is prescriptive in nature. A consultant using this approach might make these statements to the teacher who was concerned about the student who never completed work: "Here are some questions/issues that need to be addressed," or "Here are some options that need to be considered." Other questions and comments an authoritative consultant might ask or make are:

♦ "Let me investigate whether the student has the concepts or skills to complete work."

♦ "Have you determined if the student values or sees the relevance of completing this task?"

♦ "You will need to check the nature of the work the student does complete to determine what that tells you."

◆ "Look at what happens when the student does not complete work."

◆ "I will meet with the student to discuss why he or she is not completing work, then we will discuss some possible interventions."

Consultants using the authoritative approach do not share the same responsibilities as consultees (as in the collaborative approach). Their primary responsibility is to lead the problem-solving process and share their expertise with consultees. They also do not share accountability for the outcomes because consultees typically make the final decision about what plans will ultimately be implemented. During and after a problem-solving meeting, consultees have the responsibility to participate in good faith and consider the options suggested (Conoley & Conoley, 1982), implement with integrity the plan to which they agreed, and follow up and provide feedback regarding the results.

We are all familiar with the authoritative approach in our non-professional lives. It is our typical interaction with our doctors and lawyers. They do the assessment and recommend a strategy; we decide if and when we will do it. If we agree to their recommendations, we implement them in good faith and provide critical feedback. We do not share the same responsibilities and they are not accountable for the decisions we make independent of them.

Authoritative consulting has typically been the role of school psychologists, curriculum and/or special area consultants, staff developers and/or inservice trainers, special educators and related services. This approach is used because, generally, both the consultants and consultees believe that the consultants have special knowledge that is not generally known to most consultees. Consultees therefore feel it is the responsibility of consultants to assess and provide possible solutions, as well as evaluate their overall effectiveness. In its simplest form the attitude has generally been, "You figure out the problem and I will implement your solution."

The long-term effectiveness of this approach regularly comes under rigorous review because often the consultee does not feel the ownership that is required for success. However, it *is* a legitimate approach and has its rightful place in consultation. It is not unusual for consultees to request the help of people whom they believe have the skills to get the job done or, at least, can provide them with new knowledge or insights that they may not have been able to gain on their own.

The authoritative approach is most appropriate when: (1) the problem initiator does not have much knowledge about the issue or problem and is truly seeking new or more information; (2) it is obvious that a person is limited in his or her ability to identify or solve the problem or develop an appropriate plan; and (3) it is a crisis situation and the person needs advice immediately.

The authoritative approach has some downside risks and therefore should be used cautiously and appropriately. It can, in some situations:

♦ Create a "superior me works with inferior you" relationship.

♦ Increase dependency on the consultant and, as a result, decrease self-sufficiency on the part of the problem initiator.

♦ Lower the self-esteem of the problem initiator.

♦ If not done with vigilance, leave the impression that the consultant cares more about solving the problem than the person experiencing the problem.

♦ If the roles and responsibilities are not clarified, hold the consultant responsible for the failure of a program.

The authoritative approach works best when: (1) problem initiators have the option of and feel comfortable with accepting or rejecting any recommendations or findings proposed by consultants; and (2) consultants go beyond simply offering possible solutions, that is, they make every effort to teach consultees how they think about problems and how they determine appropriate solutions. This information empowers others in that it allows them to problem solve more independently in the future. Over the course of a consulting relationship, consultants can then move away from the authoritative approach toward more collaborative and facilitative approaches.

SUCCESS THROUGH FLEXIBILITY

Your skills with all three interactive approaches will significantly influence how you are likely to work with colleagues. Obviously, the wider the range of skills in your repertoire, the more successful you are likely to be. Successful consultants use the approaches fluidly and adaptively in each situation.

Sometimes people have a strong preference for or feel more comfortable using one particular approach more than another. While all approaches are appropriate, depending upon the circumstances, it is also true that some approaches can be overused or misused. If you prefer an authoritative approach and use it most of the time, it is important to remember two things: (1) you must listen *to the person*, not just the facts, before you lead, and (2) you cannot lead a parade if you get more than two blocks in front. In other words, you cannot let your earnestness and expertise distance you too much from those who seek your help. If you prefer a facilitative approach and use it most of the time, you can frustrate people who want more information on an issue or need a quick solution. For example, if someone asks you for information about alternative assessments and you respond with, "What questions are you asking yourself about alternative assessments?" they may not be too happy with your approach, no matter how appropriate it may seem to you. And, as great as collaboration is, it is not always appropriate all the time. Do you really want to collaborate (have joint responsibility) with your principal, janitor, students, or instructional aide all the time or just in those situations where it seems most appropriate?

The decision as to which interactive approach to use when consulting depends on a number of factors that include:

1. The nature of the problem.

2. The purpose of the contact.

3. The demands of the situation.

4. The amount of time available for problem solving or planning.

5. The knowledge and skills of the consultee.

6. The process skills of the consultant.

7. The interpersonal style of the consultee.

8. The interpersonal style of the consultant. (Interpersonal styles are discussed in detail in Chapters 6, 7, and 8.)

When consulting, it is possible, and probably more typical, to use a facilitative approach during some stages of the process, a collaborative approach during other stages, and an authoritative approach when it is clearly appropriate. Like teaching, it is a constant judgment call on your part.

In some consulting relationships, you may choose to begin with a facilitative approach. If goals and personal needs are being met, you would continue with this approach. If it seems apparent that the problem initiator needs a more active partner or if he or she requests a more active partner in assessment and planning, you could move to a collaborative approach. And if the problem initiator is clearly seeking information or, in your expert opinion, obviously needs additional information, you would use an authoritative approach.

In other consulting relationships, you may choose to begin with an authoritative/expert approach because it is clear that you alone have the required information or skills. As the consultee develops more expertise (from your expert modeling), you would move to a more collaborative approach. Eventually, you may select a facilitative approach with this same person because you now share similar expertise.

The skills and knowledge consultees have about the different approaches that can be used when consulting can significantly impact the success of the interaction. The more information consultees have, the more they are able to be actively involved in selecting which approach would work best for them and their specific issue or situation. For example, a teacher might request that you use a facilitative approach as he or she tries to determine the goals and purposes of a program, a collaborative approach to develop the program, and an authoritative approach to evaluate the effectiveness of the program.

Empowerment should be the ultimate goal of all consulting relationships. It should be an important consideration no matter which approach or combination of approaches are selected. Consulting, at its best, is mutually beneficial for all parties and the outcomes are increased independence. Therefore, it is a very powerful form of staff development.

THE MESSAGE

There are a number of ways to interact when communicating and problem solving with friends and colleagues. You can use a facilitative approach, a collaborative approach, an authoritative approach, or a combination of these approaches. They are all good. The key to success when consulting is to remain flexible and adaptive. The more you know about each approach, the more you can select the most appropriate approach for each situation.

4

IF YOU CAN LISTEN TO WHAT THEY TELL YOU, AND ACCEPT HOW IT SEEMS TO THEM, THEN IT IS LIKELY THAT YOU CAN WORK WITH THEM.

LISTENING TO COLLEAGUES

How do I hear the words?
How do I hear the message?

et us hear it for listening! How about three silent cheers for all the great listeners of the world? Who are they? Do you know people who are great listeners? Why do you think they are great listeners? What do they do that gives them this reputation? Why are people attracted to them? What feelings do they communicate? How do you feel when you are with them? What listening skills would you like to learn from them?

It is estimated that 80% of our waking hours is spent just listening, yet few of us have developed this skill to a high degree of sophistication. We try our best, but often we do not even know the basic tools for listening. As a result, listening skills are not readily available to us when we need them. Listening, by itself, is believed to be the most effective tool for developing relationships (trust) and influencing others.

Listening is the nexus of successful consulting. It is the stuff of change. It is the stuff of learning. Listening permeates the entire problem-solving process from establishing trust to making decisions. It is the glue that binds the process. Because of its importance and the number of skills involved, this chapter will focus solely on what good listeners do when they collaborate with colleagues.

Chapter 5 will focus exclusively on the skills for expressing yourself in a way that others will want to listen.

An inherent problem with reading about listening skills is that when listening, only about 10% of the message is carried through words, while the remaining 90% is communicated nonverbally through voice pitch, intonation, timing, facial expressions, and body language—all areas that are not accessible through the printed page. It spite of this major barrier, we shall communicate as best we can through this medium. You may have to use your imagination at times or draw upon your personal experiences to create more meaning.

LISTENING IS A GIFT

Listening is a skill you learn, and a gift you give. Good listening requires emotional strength. It involves patience, openness (being nonjudgmental), and an intense desire to understand information from another point of view. These are all highly developed qualities of character (Covey, 1989). Covey (1989) tells us, "It is so much easier to operate from a low emotional level and give high level advice" (p. 37).

People enjoy speaking and spending time with good listeners. They communicate an interest in you and a sincere desire to understand you and your world. Good listeners:

- ◆ Seek the story in the stranger. They hear what you are not saying.

- ◆ Honor you, affirm you, validate you, and make you feel important. Good listeners communicate caring; they care about who you are and what you have to say. They allow you to feel safe emotionally.

- ◆ Are empathic; they listen from their heart.

- ◆ Suspend judgment; they listen from your frame of reference and show interest in your point of view.

◆ Are positive listeners. They smile, nod their head, make affirmative sounds that acknowledge and encourage, lean forward, maintain contact, and stay focused on you.

◆ Shadow and track you. They never get too far behind, nor do they get too far in front of you. If you suddenly make a sharp turn, they stay right with you. Good listeners keep pace with you.

◆ Listen comfortably at two levels: intellectually for meaning and emotionally for feelings. They can merge the two to create a more accurate picture of your story.

◆ Are empathic, not sympathetic. When you are sympathetic, you feel sorry for someone; you pity them. This can be perceived as a form of judgment. Sympathy communicates that you do not believe that they have the power or endurance to better their lives without your help, while empathy empowers people.

◆ Use powerful listening skills. They paraphrase, clarify, reflect, and check their perceptions. They use these skills with a sincere desire to understand, not simply in a mechanistic fashion.

WHAT DO POOR LISTENERS DO?

Poor listeners are the polar opposite of good listeners. Here is how you might recognize them. You may even know some of them. Perhaps they live in your community. Poor listeners:

◆ Do not track the conversation, they stalk it! They anxiously wait for those precious opportunities to "jump in" and share their view of reality. They look for those moments when they can jump in and correct your faulty thinking (For your own good, of course!). They hurl boomerangs into the conversation whenever they can. Boomerangs are takeaway statements; they take attention away from what is being said to an obscure or unrelated comment. Boomerangs throw the speaker off; they cause the speaker to lose his or her place or thought. This is often done with oblique comments or puns. The results are that the speaker gets confused trying to make a connection between ideas.

♦ Entertain their own thoughts or prepare their rebuttal while you are talking with them. They do not squelch the urge to interrupt or to give advice. In fact, they prescribe their answers for everyone else.

♦ Read their own autobiography into your story (Covey, 1989). They listen from their frame of reference. Without realizing what they are doing, they will often make comments such as:

  - "I know how you feel. The exact same thing happened to ME."
  - "I have got to tell you what happened to ME! You will appreciate it."
  - "We have a lot in common. Let ME explain."

They filter everything you say through their own experiences, rather than making every effort to understand your experiences.

♦ Engage in annoying behaviors while you are talking with them. They fidget, squirm, look doubtful, do something else as you talk to them, try to finish your sentences, top everything you say, or worst of all, tell you that "You should not feel that way."

♦ Have a tendency to either judge, evaluate, disapprove, criticize, ridicule, contradict, or reject the message they are hearing. They listen selectively, filtering out that which they are not ready to hear. Poor listeners respond to your words with a verbal or nonverbal message that says:

  - "You are wrong about that." (editing)
  - "I wonder if that is true." (doubting)
  - "I cannot believe he is saying this." (indignantly)
  - "Can you believe it!" (sarcastically)
  - "No, I think you are wrong!" (judging)

♦ Do not quiet their inner voice that internally argues and races to conclusions. They fail to understand that such evaluative listening makes people defensive and cautious, which in turn, decreases the probability of effective communication.

♦ Find it difficult to acknowledge that another person may be right from his or her point of view. They find it difficult to suspend judgment and empathize with your situation. They fail to understand that it is not necessary to agree with the content of your message, but it is necessary to view the world through your senses and experiences.

♦ Pride themselves in being able to repeat every word a person has said. They fail to understand that if you concentrate too much on the words, you are likely to miss the message—a combination of a person's words, feelings, and behaviors.

♦ Do not have an intellectual problem, they have an emotional problem. They lack the desire to be tuned in to what people are saying. Think about this situation as an example: For many people, if they were required to take a course in parachute packing, it would probably be very boring, especially for those who have no intention of ever jumping out of a plane. The instructor would probably complain endlessly about severe attention problems among the participants. However, if he or she were to tell them that tomorrow every one of them would be forced to pack their own parachutes and jump from an airplane, their attention and listening skills would increase significantly without any training. Clearly, our needs influence the quality of our listening.

♦ Pretend to listen. They use listening skills in a mechanistic fashion. They paraphrase and clarify without communicating a sincere desire to understand. As a result, colleagues feel insulted, manipulated, and suspicious. They sense the insincerity and do not want to deal with these people. Unfortunately, these powerful communication tools develop a bad reputation when misused, and make communication difficult for people who use them appropriately and skillfully.

GOOD LISTENING IS TOUGH LISTENING

More and more information is coming at you at the speed of light. You have to be constantly prepared to multiprocess. You need to have hypersensitive listening skills, especially during the tough times. Tough times are when you find yourself in situations where you must hear what people are really saying—their message—if you want to influence their beliefs, feelings, and behavior. The following scenes are examples of those times when your listening skills are put to the test. Tough listening is:

- ♦ When a colleague dumps a bucket of objections all over your guaranteed-cure intervention kit. To add to the difficulty, none of the objections have a smattering of validity. But you listen as he or she continues.

- ♦ When a colleague berates your values, plucking away at everything you hold near and dear. The only thing that restrains you is knowing that if you openly defend yourself now, he or she will not listen to you later.

- ♦ Letting a colleague rip apart your favorite student in the lounge when many teachers are listening. To add to your challenge, other teachers are sympathizing with him or her for having to tolerate such a creep. You love that kid and you listen for the right moment to say something, but it probably will not be today. You go home heartsick.

- ♦ When a colleague misjudges your motivations and accuses you of deliberately causing a fruitless conflict. It is not true and you feel stabbed by each word as he or she finishes the tirade. Your first reaction is to strike back even though you know that that will not fix the situation, but good listening will.

- ♦ Sitting in a student conference as everyone focuses on a student's limitations with no attention being paid to his or her strengths. They are vehement about putting him or her away with students of his kind. You are adamantly opposed, and you have done all your homework to prove them wrong. But you listen and try to hear from their point of view because you know that lashing out at them and cutting their rationale to bits will not put them in your camp. However, empathic listening and patient questions may.

♦ When you are in a meeting and your brain is sizzling with great ideas on how all the problems can be solved. You wrestle down an uncontrollable urge to jump in and show your brilliance. You resist an impulse to lean forward and perch on the edge of your chair, cueing others of your impatience. You know you could jump in and win the talking contest, but you also know that you would lose that golden opportunity to integrate everyone's ideas into a creative plan in which all can feel a sense of ownership.

In each one of these difficult listening scenarios, people are sending loud messages about how they are feeling and what their needs are. Messages are communicated primarily through nonverbal behaviors (e.g., facial expressions, gestures, eye contact, physical stance, loudness of voice). The diversity of avenues a listener has for collecting information is unlimited and intense. Several of them together, not just a single one, communicate feelings. Until people feel certain that you have heard their message, it is impossible for them to listen to you.

NONVERBAL LISTENING

Nonverbal behaviors that we use when listening are the conduit for emotional messages. These habituated behavioral patterns are learned over a period of time and people generally have no awareness that they are using them. Because of this, it is difficult to deceive others with words because all our nonverbal behaviors reveal our true feelings. For example, a person may indicate that he or she is very interested in listening to what you have to say but is constantly glancing away at the time. Which behavior would you believe? When verbal and nonverbal messages are incongruent, the listener initially is confused but usually will end up believing the nonverbal message.

Nonverbal listening is essential to understanding what people are saying. Without it, the accuracy of comprehending the information is reduced by 66% (Heese & Tepper, 1972). Studies by Mehrabian (1971) indicate that information is communicated in the following manner:

♦ 7% through words.
♦ 38% through voice pitch, intonation, and timing.
♦ 55% through facial expressions and body language.

Example: A person's actual words might simply be, "Oh, yeah." As you read them or hear them stated in a monotone voice, they communicate very little. At best, they acknowledge that your words were heard. However, when voice quality and body language are included, these two simple words are able to communicate a range of human emotions: boredom, excitement, interest, doubt, anger, and threat.

It is nearly impossible for you to identify the real message in any of the difficult listening scenarios presented earlier because you had to be there at the time it was happening if you wanted to hear more than just the words.

FACILITATIVE LISTENING SKILLS

Facilitative listening is an active process. It communicates to the speaker that you are with them. It is a deliberate attempt to hear all verbal and nonverbal cues being sent, from the person, the environment, and within oneself. Active listening is total listening.

Facilitative listening is hard work. It involves both *attending* and *responding* skills. Initially, as you are learning these skills, you may sound a little mechanistic, but people will forgive and overlook this if they sense that you have a sincere desire to understand.

Facilitative listening takes time. It takes time to check in regularly with the speaker as you are communicating. But the investment of time up front is worth it because, in the long run, it saves time. You rarely have to go back and redo things, correct misunderstandings, or repair a damaged relationship.

Attending skills

Attending skills are the nonverbal behaviors you use while listening. Even without words, you still communicate a clear message to colleagues that you are sincerely interested in them as fellow human beings. Attending behavior is a powerful tool for influencing others. Attending skills include these accepting behaviors:

- ◆ Body orientation
- ◆ Eye contact
- ◆ Facial expressions
- ◆ Gesturing
- ◆ Touching
- ◆ Facing fully
- ◆ Leaning forward
- ◆ Focusing and resisting distractions
- ◆ Waiting to respond
- ◆ Observing cues

Responding skills

Responding skills are behaviors that you use as you are listening as well. The act of responding includes both verbal and nonverbal behaviors. Their purpose is to:

- ◆ Encourage people to continue sharing their thoughts.
- ◆ Check the accuracy of the message being sent.
- ◆ Help people feel comfortable revealing their thoughts and feelings.

Responding skills become increasingly more complex as you attempt to check the accuracy of the message that is being communicated between the speaker and you, the listener. They can be as simple as nodding your head or using minimal encouragers such as "Mm-hm," and "Go on, I am listening." The more complex skills include:

- ◆ Paraphrasing
- ◆ Clarifying
- ◆ Reflecting

◆ Perception checking

The most critical feature of these facilitative skills is that they do not add to or editorialize on what has been said, yet, they do not leave anything out.

PARAPHRASING

Paraphrasing is accomplished when you restate, in a simplified form, the beliefs, thoughts, and stated feelings of the speaker in an effort to check their accuracy. After you have submitted a tentative synthesis (the essence) of a person's ideas, it is the speaker's responsibility to approve, modify, or clarify your paraphrase. Here is an example:

> *Statement:*   "What is the use of trying to help these kids!"
>
> *Paraphrase:*   "You think that these kids cannot be helped."

The speaker can respond to the accuracy of the paraphrase by either confirming or correcting it, such as:

> *Confirmation:* "That is right, I do not think they can."
>
> *Correction:*   "No, I just feel discouraged right now."

When you paraphrase, it allows people to listen to themselves by providing a mirror of their ideas, thoughts, and stated feelings. In the last example, you can see the importance of paraphrasing before you continue: what the person said may not be what he or she meant. Paraphrases often begin with these phrases:

◆ "What you are saying is . . . ."
◆ "You believe . . . ."
◆ "It seems to you . . . ."
◆ "Your sense is . . . ."

There is no judgment. Every attempt is made to match the person's statement with the same or similar words.

CLARIFYING

Clarifying occurs when you, as the listener, ask a person to explain more clearly the message he or she is expressing. It usually takes the form of a question:

Statement: "What is the use of trying to help these kids!"

Clarification: "Are you saying that these kids cannot be helped?"

The question is a genuine search for clarity, not a judgment of the statement. You must be extremely careful about keeping the non-verbal message you are sending congruent with your question. Voice pitch and intonation, as well as facial expressions and body language, can change a genuine question into a heavily laden judgmental remark. Try restating the question with different intonations and hear the difference.

REFLECTING

Reflecting attempts to provide a true mirror of a person's deepest feelings. Reflecting is a very difficult skill to learn because it demands deeply empathic listening and understanding. It brings to the surface and expresses in words the feelings that lie behind the person's words. It is almost impossible to write a reflective statement because the written word carries no feeling. The following is a modest attempt:

Statement: "What is the use of trying to help these kids!"

Reflection: "You are really frustrated with these students."

You try to capture the person's feelings. The speaker now can either confirm or correct your reflective statement:

Confirmation: "I really am!"

Correction: "No, I think I am just tired. I will feel better about this tomorrow."

A reflection focuses on the emotional message, not just the content, that is being revealed. Reflection can be a very self-revealing tool for the person who is speaking because it captures their feeling tone. Often people are unaware of their real feelings and they would not have brought them to the surface had it not been for your help as a listener.

PERCEPTION CHECKING

Perception checking is very similar to reflecting feelings. It is the flip side. Instead of making a statement that reflects what you sense a person is feeling, you check your perceptions of their feelings by asking a question. It also requires deep empathic listening and understanding. The following is an attempt at creating a perception checking example:

> *Statement:*   "What is the use of trying to help these kids!"

> *Perception* *check:*   "You sound really frustrated with these students, are you?"

You check the person's feelings by posing a tentative question. The speaker now can either confirm or correct your perception check:

> *Confirmation:* "I really am. Thanks for hearing it."

> *Correction:*   "No, I think I am just irritated. This, too, shall pass."

Like reflection, a perception check focuses on the emotional message, not just the content, that is being revealed by the speaker.

LEADING STRATEGIES

Communication begins with facilitative skills like attending and responding. They are most appropriate during the early phases of consulting. Later in the process, as you work more collaboratively, you may choose to use more persuasive techniques. These are called leading strategies (Benjamin, 1981). Until now, the consultee's ideas and feelings have been the *only* focus. When you begin to lead, you get yourself actively involved by putting yourself on stage with the consultee. Your frame of reference now comes into focus in your mutual effort to create a more desired outcome.

The danger in using leading strategies is the possibility of taking over the process at the expense of the consultee. Some consultants find that the limitation of self during the initial stages, when they are only using attending and responding skills, is very difficult and not enough for them. In fact, they find it downright uncongenial. Consequently, they make the mistake of leaping into the process much too early with their points of view and their own solutions. When this happens, the consultee is left with the feeling that this is just another spectator sport.

You cannot lead until you thoroughly listened. You cannot lead until you have established a high degree of trust. People are not ready to share their stage with you until they believe in their solar plexus that you have their best interests at heart, not just your own. There are several leading strategies that we can use to influence and persuade:

- ◆ Interpreting
- ◆ Explaining
- ◆ Encouraging
- ◆ Assuring
- ◆ Suggesting
- ◆ Agreeing/Disagreeing
- ◆ Challenging
- ◆ Humoring

As you learn about these strategies, it will become evident that each one has its strengths and limitations (Benjamin, 1981). It is their limitations that can be an impediment, so be careful. Use with caution.

Interpreting

When interpreting, you go beyond simple feedback and reflection to presenting an alternative frame of reference or another point of view for consideration. The essential difference between leading and facilitating is that you are now redefining reality from your perspective, instead of reflecting only how it seems to the consultee. Interpretations might sound like this:

- ♦ "I am wondering from what you have said if we should use alternative assessments."
- ♦ "It seems to me that cooperative teaching is not going well for you this year."
- ♦ "It sounds like you are finding it difficult to accept her lack of progress, given your effort."

When you interpret, you suggest or offer your opinion about a situation which, of course, can be confirmed or corrected by the consultee.

Explaining

An explanation is a neutral, matter-of-fact, descriptive statement that explains how things really are. Explanations can be used at the beginning of a meeting to explain your position and/or a colleague's position, or it can be used in response to statements or questions. Here are some examples:

- ♦ "I know that this is a difficult situation for you but we cannot entertain the possibility of removing Jan from her current educational environment until we have documented evidence of systematic, ongoing attempts to solve the problem."

- ♦ "Here is the picture I get. I am not stating absolutely that my observations are 100% accurate; I am only describing how it appears to me. Students need power and control. They will do anything to get it. When you consistently make all the decisions for them, they rebel."

- ♦ (To an administrator) "Let me explain my position. I cannot work with Ms. Day until she decides that she has a need to do this. If you want me to work with her, it may be necessary for you to structure the environment in order to create the need."

All of these statements imply that there is no other choice, one must accept them and act accordingly.

Encouraging

Encouraging is a lead that is expressed verbally and openly. You encourage by offering support and reinforcement to colleagues for their efforts to change in a direction that you believe is in everyone's best interest. For instance:

- ♦ "I am impressed with your tenacity."
- ♦ "You certainly have been trying to implement a number of different strategies this year."
- ♦ "I want to commend you for including Miguel in the reading group. I know it is difficult to do."

Again, use these strategies with caution. As you can see, these comments can make you sound just a bit superior.

Assuring

Assuring is a lead that tells a person that you believe in his or her ability to solve the problem and, because it is being approached collaboratively, you are doubly confident. A few examples are:

- ♦ "Fortunately, these kinds of problems are your bailiwick."
- ♦ "If anyone can manage this situation, it is you."
- ♦ "I am sure that we can solve this problem together.

This lead is an attempt to build confidence and encourage the person to take risks.

Suggesting

Suggesting is a mild form of advice giving, so use it very cautiously. No one likes to be told what to do even when they ask, so do not be fooled into giving too much advice.

A suggestion must be presented as one equal talking to another equal, one of whom may possess more information or experience on a particular subject. Its overtone must be tentative. It cannot imply that a colleague should comply; it is presented only as an idea that might work, or something to think about. It is up to the person to decide on its utility. Examples of suggesting might be:

- ◆ "Here is an idea I think may work, but you may be in a better position to decide if it is possible."

- ◆ "I am wondering what would happen if we tried this strategy."

- ◆ "Let me think aloud about a couple of possibilities. Then we can talk about what sounds possible to you."

As you can see, the purpose of this approach is to stimulate a colleague to consider additional possibilities.

Agreeing/Disagreeing

Agreeing or disagreeing is a lead that you use to communicate whether the consultee is right or wrong. This, of course, is presented in the context of your own experiences and training. It is only your opinion from your frame of reference and it needs to be clearly stated as such. This is especially necessary if you are expressing a value judgment about a particular issue or behavior. For example:

- ◆ "The data, as well as everything you have told me, leads me to believe that your plan should work."

- ◆ "I cannot envision how that strategy would work in this situation. But I can appreciate the pressure you must be feeling to do something now, right or wrong."

- ◆ "I believe the reading program you selected is a better choice because of its emphasis on comprehension."

All of these comments involve value judgments, so use with caution!

Challenging

Challenging is making a constructive, growth-producing statement that forces a person to question, reexamine, then possibly modify some aspect of his or her behavior, feelings, or beliefs. Challenges can be presented as informational feedback, discrepancy feedback, or a confrontation of a hidden agenda:

◆ *Informational*: "I noticed when you call on Norman to answer a question, your facial expressions and body language change. I sense your irritation with him. I am wondering if Norman or the other students notice it. Would it help to see yourself on videotape?"

◆ *Discrepancy*: "Earlier, I heard you say that nothing was working and you are ready to throw in the towel. But I see from your monitoring data that students have made some positive growth. Can you help me understand this?"

◆ *Confrontation of a hidden agenda*: "My sense is that you are not so much interested in using my help to adapt the science program as you are in finding helpful resources outside the class."

How growth-producing any challenge is depends to a large extent on a variety of intrapersonal and interpersonal factors:

◆ The consultee's sense of self-worth and self-esteem.
◆ Your interpersonal style.
◆ The consultee's interpersonal style.
◆ The consultee's acceptance of feedback.
◆ The trust established between you.
◆ Your manner of presentation: Is it tentative or absolute?
◆ Your motives: Do you want to genuinely help? (You can hurt if your intent is to set people straight on their erroneous beliefs.)

When challenging statements are made with a superior attitude, they can be destructive to a relationship. Any time you elicit defensive reactions such as counterattacking, avoiding, or escaping, it is best to retreat because the encounter has become unproductive.

Be aware of your attitudes toward a consultee prior to challenging him or her. Be sure they are not the primary motivation for your challenging statements.

Humoring

Before concluding this section on leading strategies, one more deserves mention: humoring. Its purpose is to ease tension and possibly to create a genuine bond between you and consultees. It can be in the form of an anecdote or a poignant remark that elicits laughter and enjoyment. The situation, the people involved, the issue, and the timing determine its success. Humoring should:

♦ Be spontaneous and natural.
♦ Stem from empathic listening.
♦ Reflect a positive outlook on things.

It is very difficult (and very risky) to give examples of humoring in a brief statement because, as was stated, it is so situational and person-dependent, but here is a modest attempt:

♦ "This is difficult but I'm sure we can figure this out. Between the two of us, we should have a total of 280 IQ points—my 80 and your 200."

♦ "They say that mistakes are a part of learning. If that's true, we should be getting gold stars!"

♦ "Given our hardships to date, I should not be surprised to hear the board announce that due to current financial restraints, the lights at the end of the tunnel will be turned off until further notice."

QUESTIONABLE PERSUASIVE STRATEGIES

There are a number of leading strategies that should be avoided except as last resort and, even then, it is questionable if they should ever be used at all (Benjamin, 1981). They all imply superiority or coercion. What follows are questionable leads that consultants often misuse.

Advice giving

Advice giving, essentially, is telling someone what to do, when to do it, and why he or she should. For example:

> ♦ "You need to let the student know who is in control and you ought to do it right away, otherwise she will run all over you."

Advice giving has many limitations. First, it often is meaningless to the person and rarely applied unless he or she is ready to understand and to see its benefits. Think of how much inservice training is useless because there is not a match between what the speaker is saying and what the participants need to know at this point in their teaching careers. Secondly, some people would rather give advice freely than get involved in the struggles of another person. Collaborative problem solving takes time. Giving advice is easy—usually wrong—but fast and easy.

A third reason to avoid advice giving is that you are trapped in a catch-22. If you give advice that works, you create dependency. Consultees return for more and more of your profound wisdom. As they glow with gratitude, you feel honored. It is highly reinforcing. If you give advice that does not work, you are awarded full blame and responsibility, and you now are expected to generate pearls of wisdom of even better quality. Some people can seek your advice earnestly only to prove that it is worthless and, by implication, you are worthless. Giving advice sets you up to be rejected and depressed when your expert advice or opinions are not used.

There are situations where advice giving can prove useful but it must be approached correctly. For example, if a consultee earnestly is seeking your advice and you are sure that there is a readiness, then you may choose to do so. However, do not comply immediately to their request, but rather seek information about what consultees think about the situation and what alternatives they have already tried. Then qualify your advice by indicating that you do not have their experiences or frame of reference but, from your frame of reference, here is how you see it or what you might do. (Remember the problems of Reta and Tom in Chapter 1?)

Always give the responsibility back by encouraging colleagues to think it through for themselves and to decide for themselves what fits best for them. Once in a while, if you are lucky, you find the right words that crystallize their thoughts. You say what they are thinking, and probably were going to do without your advice.

Urging

Urging is used to prod or cajole people to do what, in your opinion, is best for them. It is an attempt to spur them into action when they seem hesitant to budge. For example:

> ♦ "Of course you can! It is not that difficult to design. Let us try it now."

At times, urging has positive results. Your support and confidence in their ability may be timely and sufficient to mobilize them.

Moralizing

Moralizing is a mixture of advice giving, urging, and conscience-beating. You use their conscience, yours, and Everyman's. It brings into play those sacred, social norms that no one in his or her right sense would dare to oppose and, if he or she did, the punishment is guilt. For example:

> ♦ "I do not understand how you can feel that way! Jon really likes you and he tries to do his very best to please you. When he tries so hard, you ought to make every attempt to encourage and support him. [In a placating voice] You probably are just having a rough week and really do not feel that way generally. Right?"

If you are victorious with moralizing, examine at what price your victory has been won. People respond in several ways:

> ♦ They become more cautious so as not to get trapped again.
> ♦ They submit but become bitter and discouraged.
> ♦ They become shrewd and try to outwit you.

◆ They only appear to comply, temporarily disarming you only to get you later.

At best, moralizing provides feedback to others about how you think society is likely to judge them.

Disbelief

Disbelief implies that the consultee's perceptions of a situation obviously are incorrect or distorted and that yours are more objective. For example:

◆ "I cannot believe you feel that way! Especially, not you! I thought you always saw the best in everyone."

Would this statement make you change your behavior, or just make you feel guilty and awful?

Sarcasm

Sarcasm condescendingly communicates how absurd and unacceptable a consultee's perceptions are. For example:

◆ "Surely you do not think I need to be here every time Susan has a problem! Retardation is not a communicable disease; she can work cooperatively with others."

Through sarcasm, you hope to shake the person free from the ridiculous perceptions that he or she holds. It implies, "If you think like me, you will be fine!"

Contradicting

Contradicting asserts that the consultee definitely is wrong and there are not two ways of viewing the situation. For example:

◆ "No. Wrong! This is how it is done. First, you confront the student, then you tell him what his options are."

It implies no doubt. You are convinced that your way is the right way, the best way, and the only way.

INAPPROPRIATE PERSUASIVE STRATEGIES

Some leading strategies can be downright obnoxious and therefore should be avoided at all costs (even if it will make you feel better for a fleeting moment). These "extreme" leading strategies include rejecting, scolding, threatening, punishing, and ordering. None of these will be discussed here as they are self-explanatory.

All of the leading strategies discussed in the last section and the ones listed above are either of questionable effectiveness or are obviously unacceptable. The sad reality is that many of us, in our sincere efforts to get things done, use many of them. To make matters worse, we use them without conscious awareness. However, these questionable and unacceptable practices do not escape their victim's awareness—the person with whom you seek to work collaboratively.

In summary, some leading strategies can be used effectively when working collaboratively. They are more directly persuasive than the facilitative skills of attending or responding. The key to their success is that you have completely listened to the consultee's views and have used the leading strategies skillfully and sincerely. As a consultant, you need to be keenly aware of the following factors:

  ♦ When you are leading.
  ♦ Whom you are leading.
  ♦ For what purpose you are leading.

Additionally, you must communicate clearly to colleagues that they are always free to accept or reject your leads without fear of offending you. A climate of trust is a necessary prerequisite to leading. (See also *The Helping Interview* (1981) by Alfred Benjamin, for a more extensive study of each of the leading strategies reviewed in this chapter.)

THE MESSAGE

Good listening is not easy. It is one of the most difficult skills to acquire. But, when achieved, it has the highest potential for developing quality relationships and influencing others. Listening occurs at two levels: hearing the words that are used and hearing the message that is intended. Hearing the message is the highest level of listening because it identifies emotional needs, not just content. People trust people who hear what they are feeling.

Some leading strategies, used knowingly and skillfully, can yield benefits in a trusting, collaborative relationship. They are especially useful when it becomes clear that you must move beyond attending and responding to effect the change you feel is necessary. Some leading strategies should be avoided because of the risk they pose to developing and maintaining a working relationship.

5

**SPEAKING
WITH COLLEAGUES**

*How do I invite people to listen?
How do I ask inviting questions?*

CHANGE OCCURS AS A DIRECT RESULT OF THOSE RARE INDIVIDUALS WHO CAN EXPRESS THEMSELVES IN A WAY THAT OTHERS WANT TO LISTEN.

If you really want to be understood, you have to work at it. One should not be surprised if misunderstood; a natural result of communication is misunderstanding. Why? Because words are symbols. They are not the real thing. We all have had many different experiences with the same symbols. For example, when you hear the word "phone," what do you see? Is it beige? Is it portable? Is it a cellular? Is it touch tone? What shape is it? Is your image of a telephone likely to look exactly like mine? What is the probability that it would be identical? Similarly, if you heard a colleague say that someone's home was gorgeous, would you envision the same image as she saw? Not likely. Your concept of a gorgeous home may be completely different from what your colleague liked. When you think about it—if only one or two simple little words can result in miscommunication, can you imagine what an entire sentence might do?

Anyone who wants to be heard accurately must take as much responsibility for delivering a clear message as the listener must take for receiving the message accurately. It is not just what you say (the content) that needs to be examined carefully but, equally important, the way you deliver your message (the process). Communication experts believe more attention should be paid to the process than the content.

By definition, effective communication requires the expression of an idea, a belief, a need, or a feeling by a speaker and the assimilation of this information by a listener in such a way that there is an almost perfect correspondence between what the speaker intended to say and what the listener understood. No small or easy task!

Communication is much more complex, however, than one person talking while the other is listening. Communication is dynamic and interactive. At its best, it is messy! To help you communicate better, this chapter will focus on the role and skills of the speaker in the communication process. For our purposes, the speaker is the person who is talking with a colleague about his or her ideas, beliefs, opinions, needs, and feelings. Our speaker is not a person who is talking at us or not involving us in a conversation, as might be the case when a person is delivering a speech. In an effort to communicate even more clearly, we shall refer to the speaker in this chapter as the communicator.

COMMUNICATION IS DIFFICULT

Let us continue exploring miscommunication. Instead of limiting ourselves to single words as we did earlier, let us really complicate the process by examining three relatively simple sentences:

♦ "This at-risk student is immature."
♦ "The administration is uncooperative."
♦ "Teacher, I cleaned my desk."

What is the likelihood that we would all agree upon what at-risk or immature means? Who makes up administration? What do they *do* when they are uncooperative? What does clean mean? Is the teacher's vision of a clean desk likely to match the student's? What is your image of a desk? Because most communication extends far beyond a sentence, can you imagine a conversation over the span of an hour (or a lifetime)?

Communication is difficult because it occurs on a minimum of three levels:

1. What the speaker is saying.

2. What the speaker thinks he or she is saying.

3. What the listener thinks the speaker is saying.

With all the potential breakdowns, one feels fortunate to be understood at all.

Communication is difficult because you must express yourself honestly and openly if you want your listener to hear your intended message. Honestly and openly means that you have to take risks and communicate your feelings as well as your thoughts. This is not easy for several reasons:

1. You often do not feel free to say what you are feeling and thinking.

2. You may be unaware of your real feelings at the time.

3. Feelings are difficult to capture in words—it is like trying to describe the Grand Canyon to a person who is blind.

As you can see, there are as many difficulties in communicating a clear message as there are in receiving a message accurately.

WHAT DO GOOD COMMUNICATORS DO?

Before we explore this topic, think of someone with whom you enjoy having a conversation. Now recall a conversation that you have had with this person recently. As you visualize it, ask yourself what were the effective tools and behaviors this person was using? Would you describe your star communicator in the following way? Good communicators:

◆ Engage you. They invite you into their world. They capture your attention. They bring you into the conversation without your conscious awareness. They involve you.

◆ Make what they say relevant to you and your world. You understand them. You can relate to their experiences.

◆ Share a part of themselves with you. Without seeming to do so, they say, "Here is who I am."

◆ Build rapport even when they are reporting information. They are constantly tuned in to you.

◆ Value you as a listener. They check in with you frequently. They are interested in how their information is being received. They need to know if you are both on the same wavelength.

◆ Encourage you to provide feedback. They want you to paraphrase and reflect what you hear. That is how they monitor the accuracy of their message. They intermittently say things such as:

- "Tell me what you hear me saying."
- "Clarify for me what I just said."
- "Am I making sense to you?"
- "Have I said this before?"

◆ Monitor their pace. They vary their rate depending upon the complexity of the content. They give you time to integrate information as they are talking. They communicate ideas, not simply words.

When you think about it, it is difficult to understand how one could be a good communicator without first being a good listener.

WHAT POOR COMMUNICATORS DO

Most poor communicators do not have a performance deficit, they have a skill deficit. They often do not know what good communication looks or sounds like, therefore, they cannot do it. So what do poor communicators look and sound like? Poor communicators:

◆ Talk at you, not with you. They virtually ignore you as they talk. They do not appear to need you to listen. They love to hear their own stories and can talk as long as you can listen. They do not appear to have the skills to check in to see if you are even interested in what they have to say.

◆ Do not take turns. Effective communication is like a ball being tossed regularly back and forth between two people.

When poor communicators get the ball, they keep it as long as they can.

♦ Use unfamiliar acronyms, in-house language, unfamiliar words, and talk about unfamiliar characters expecting you to follow the conversation. For example:

- "Metacognitive"
- "Intraneurosensory"
- "SWAT team"

♦ Do not provide a context for their comments or stories. They seem to start the conversation on "Chapter Two" of their story and expect you to catch up.

♦ Use unnaturally long pauses between phrases. Unfortunately, as you wait patiently for every phrase or sentence, you go on a mental holiday and are frequently not there when they continue.

WHAT TO REMEMBER WHEN COMMUNICATING

Delivering a clear message involves several interrelated factors. All of them must be examined and monitored as you interact with people about your ideas, opinions, and feelings. What might you add to this list to guarantee successful interactions with your colleagues:

♦ *Your message must communicate your frame of reference, your assumptions, your intentions, and/or the conceptual leaps you are making.* For example, you may need to clarify your frame of reference at a child-study team meeting by saying something such as:

- "Here is how I view the situation. Special education is not a place or a person, it is a service. Therefore, it can occur anywhere."
- "I am assuming that we all using the basic elements of effective instruction."
- "Here is what I hope to clarify in our time together."

♦ *Create a context for what you are saying.* Provide advance organizers for listeners just as you do with students. For example:

- "There are several ways to develop collaborative work cultures. Consulting is one of them."
- "Portfolio assessments are a part of, not apart from, alternative assessments."
- "Co-teaching falls under the umbrella of service delivery models."

♦ *Your message must be appropriate to the listener's frame of reference.* People's experiential backgrounds, age, sex, race, and professional training, must be considered. You must be careful not to talk over or under people's heads. This is of particular importance during any interaction where people's experiences are likely to be significantly different: parent conferences, professional development workshops, child-study conferences, coaching, consulting, collaborative teaching, teacher assistance team meetings, etc.

♦ *Verbal and nonverbal messages must be congruent.* If you want to be understood, decrease the possibility of more confusion. Consider this conversation. You say, "Go ahead, please explain your position. I am listening." Your statement can have several different meanings depending upon your facial expressions and body language. If you are leaning forward with your arms down, facing the person, and your voice sounds inviting, your verbal and nonverbal messages are congruent. However, if you are leaning back with your arms and legs crossed, a frown on your face, with an "I doubt if you are right" tone in your voice, it is unlikely that you want to actively listen (with empathy and acceptance) to a colleague's position. When listeners are confused, they tend to follow the nonverbal message and, in this case, withdraw.

♦ *You must unambiguously communicate your feelings.* This is difficult because, as indicated earlier, emotional words have different meanings to different people based on personal experiences. To say "I feel upset," can create a plethora of images for different people. Are you physically ill or mildly annoyed? It might be a little bit clearer if you were to say, "I am angry enough to scream!" To say, "I am mad as a hatter," may not communicate how you really feel. When was the last time anyone saw a hatter, let alone a hatter who was mad? While it is difficult to communicate feelings, it is better to try to explain your feelings than not to acknowledge or discuss them at all.

◆ *Request feedback frequently regarding what message your listener is receiving.* Soliciting continuous feedback more readily assures that the listener is hearing your *intended* message. This often-quoted statement summarizes nicely the importance of feedback: "I know you believe you understand what you think I said, but I wonder if you realize that what I said is not what I meant."

◆ *Other people's actions must be described in precise, behavioral terms devoid of judgment and interpretation.* For example, it is more accurate to describe a person's behavior by saying, "She cries easily and avoids conflict," than to say the person is oversensitive. Likewise, neurosis is unclear unless you describe it by saying that the person frequently says she is worried about many things and discusses many personal fears.

◆ *Own your own messages by using personal pronouns such as "I" or "my."* Avoid statements like, "Some people say. . . ," or "Most people do . . . ." In other words, take personal responsibility for your feelings and ideas. Do not try to bring an army into the conversation to defend your opinion.

◆ *Be redundant to assure being heard.* Repeat your message again and again in different ways. Spaced repetition is one way that people hear new information and remember it over time. Advertisers use this practice very effectively. They have found that advertising pays because they carefully select a message that will penetrate our consciousness and by repeating it again and again—both verbally and visually—it becomes lodged into the subconscious.

Too often, we make the mistake of saying something once and expect people to hear it. People only hear what they are ready to hear. Unless the new information has pay-value or contains a threat, chances are very high that it was not even heard.

♦ *Avoid using jargon, abbreviated terms, or acronyms unless everyone is completely familiar with the in-house language.* It seems that each profession talks to itself in its own unique language. Apparently, there is no Rosetta Stone! Special education, particularly the field of learning disabilities, contains a plethora of very perplexing terms that can confuse and alienate people who are not trained in the field. How comfortable are people with terms like *S.L.D.* (specific learning disabilities), *B.D.* (behavioral disorders), intraneurosensory learning, perceptual-processing disorder, metacognitive strategies, reauditorization deficits, haptic modality, perseveration, and many more.

As you can see, it is not easy to be understood. It takes a conscious and concerted effort all the time. You can never assume that people understand what you are saying no matter how important it is to you.

QUESTIONING STRATEGIES

The question is one of the valuable tools we have in our communication-tools kit. Because it is an integral part of successful communications and collaborative problem solving, it behooves us all to learn how to ask the types of questions that will give us the information we want when we interact with colleagues.

All types of questions are useful and effective. The best type to use depends on the situation and your specific purpose. How you phrase your questions will affect the quality of the responses you get. So before you pose a question, think about the kind of response you want. Do you prefer a short, factual response or an information-loaded response? Each type has unique qualities and advantages. Four types of questions are discussed in this chapter:

♦ Open Questions
♦ Closed Questions
♦ Direct Questions
♦ Indirect Questions

Open and closed questions

Open questions encourage people to share a variety of views, ideas, opinions, beliefs, and feelings. Closed questions tend to focus discussion toward a specific response, usually in the form of facts or yes/no responses. Succinctly stated, the open question is broad; the closed question is narrow. The concept is exemplified in the following:

Open: "How do you feel about portfolio assess-ments?"

Closed: "You appear uneasy about portfolio assess-ments, are you?"

Open: "You seem discouraged today. What hap-pened that concerns you?"

Closed: "Are you discouraged today?"

Open: "Some people enjoy teaching at-risk stu-dents; others do not. What are your feelings?"

Closed: "Do you enjoy teaching at-risk students?"

The following are some additional examples of open questions. How would you state them so that they were closed? Give these a try:

♦ "Now that you have provided an overview of the problem, where would you like to begin?"
♦ "What can we agree to?"
♦ "How do you feel about the plan so far?"
♦ "You expressed some concerns. How can I help?"

A minor point (but major in its consequences) needs to be made about the last example. Never ask, "How can I help *you*? The word "you" connotes an inferior relationship by implying, "I am strong, you are weak; you need my help." Simply say, "How can I help?"

Here are some clues to assist you in recognizing and constructing different types of questions. Open questions generally begin with the two words: How and What. They encourage people to explain ideas and they allow for self-exploration.

Closed questions, on the other hand, usually begin with these words: When, Where, Are, Do, Have, Should, Will, and Can. There are some closed questions that are extremely closed and should be avoided if you are truly in pursuit of information. These questions either include or assume the desired responses, or coerce a colleague to agree with you. Closed questions can leave colleagues with the feeling that if they do not agree, they suffer the implied consequences—our wrath, displeasure, and rejection. The following are examples of *very* closed questions:

- ♦ "It is clear that Lee is not a truly disruptive child. Do you not agree?"

- ♦ "You surely do not believe that all students can learn using your lecture method, do you?"

- ♦ "Is it not a fact that all students have a right to be with normally-achieving peers?"

Can you recall being on the receiving end of these types of questions? How did they make you feel?

Direct and indirect questions

The second type of questions to consider using when communicating and problem solving with colleagues is the direct and indirect form. Direct questions are straight queries. They can be either open or closed. They are direct because they have a question mark at the end, and our voices go up indicating that a question has been posed for which a response is sought.

Indirect questions, on the other hand, inquire without seeming to do so. They usually have no question mark at the end, but it is clear to everyone that a question was posed and a response sought. They leave the field wide open. Note in the following examples how all the open questions are direct but how they can be made even more open by stating them indirectly. For instance:

Direct:	"How does the intervention plan seem to you?" (Open)
Indirect:	"I am curious to know how the intervention plan seems to you."

―――――

Direct:	"What do you think of the new grading system?" (Open)
Indirect:	"I am wondering what you think about the new grading system."

―――――

Direct:	"What do you suggest we do?" (Open)
Indirect:	"You probably have some ideas about how this problem might be approached."

―――――

Direct:	"It *is* difficult to plan for more than two reading groups. Is it not?" (Closed)
Indirect:	"It must be difficult having to plan for more than two reading groups."

Indirect questions frequently begin with:

◆ "I wonder how . . . ."
◆ "I am confused about . . . ."
◆ "I get the impression that . . . ."
◆ "I do not know anything about . . . ."
◆ "Share your impressions around . . . ."
◆ "Let us talk about . . . ."
◆ "My guess is that . . . ."

The question is an extremely useful tool when it is used delicately and appropriately. Because it has limitations, the fewer direct questions (open or closed) you use, the less likely you are to create a climate that implies that, my job is to ask the questions and yours is to answer them.

―――――

If you wish to study the different forms of questions, their uses and abuses, spend some time comparing the different interview styles used by the reporters on the "McNeil-Lehrer News Hour" with those used by Mike Wallace on CBS and Ted Koppel on ABC. Once you have evaluated their questioning techniques, you may want to study and self-monitor your own uses and abuses of the question.

APPROPRIATE USES FOR THE QUESTION

There are occasions when questions are necessary and appropriate; the following are eight such occasions:

1. To obtain identification or objective information, as is done during interviews.

    Example: "How many students do you have in your class?" (closed)

2. To clarify when a person is being vague or evasive.

    Example: "I am unclear with the term 'learned help-less.' Please help." (indirect)

3. To define the problem more precisely before designing interventions.

    Example: "What strategies does the student use when the content is not clear?" (open)

4. To clarify, step-by-step, a course of action that has been taken or will be taken.

    Example: "What did we agree needed to be done after we did a needs assessment?" (open)

5. To request feedback about whether you got your intent across accurately.

    Example: "I need your help. What did you understand me to say?" (open)

    "I would be interested to know what sense you made of my ambiguous remarks." (indirect)

6. To explore an important thought or feeling in more depth.

   Example: "You mentioned 'too little time,' please ex-
                 pand on that." (indirect)

7. To facilitate someone who is expressing anger and seems
   hesitant to continue.

   Example: "Anything else you need to say?" (closed,
                 but its intent is open)

                 "Please continue." (indirect)

8. To encourage others to talk when you sense there are issues
   left unstated.

   Example: "Anything else that needs to be said before
                 we continue?" (closed, but its intent is
                 open)

RESULTS OF THE INAPPROPRIATE QUESTION

The question is a basic tool in the problem-solving process. However, it may come as a surprise to you to learn that it can be abused
and, as a result, have a deleterious effect on the consulting process.
Consulting sessions should not be studded with a series of questions. Asking too many questions is a frequent error made by
novices. More is not better. When consultees find themselves
caught in a hailstorm of questions, it should come as no surprise to
see them race for the nearest shelter in their attempts to survive.
The question can appear to them to be a deadly weapon. It can be
wielded in a way that destroys trust, inhibits rapport, and damages
any attempts at collaborative problem solving. Closed questions are
the most destructive. The results of inappropriate questioning techniques may include:

♦ An intrusive question-answer pattern is created when you
   depend too much on the question as the primary form of
   gaining information instead of active listening. You leave the
   impression that your role is to ask the salient questions and
   your colleague's role is to provide the answers.

♦ When you take charge by asking all the questions, you leave your colleague with an impression of your superiority and expert authority. The message is: Only an expert knows what is important and relevant information to gather.

♦ Bombarding colleagues with a series of questions can be very intimidating and humiliating, especially if they have not anticipated them. They can be made to look stupid and incompetent. All questioning should be prefaced like this:

> "I need to ask some questions. I fully accept that it may be impossible to answer many of them at this time. But, hopefully, we can get a general idea of the problem and we can proceed from there."

The voice tone of this statement will determine the comfort level of the exchange.

♦ Continuous questioning leaves colleagues with the expectation that you have a ready-made, guaranteed solution in your bag of tricks. Otherwise, why would you have asked for so many details? They are tempted to think, "What are you good for if you are unable to pronounce a verdict after all the questioning?" Disappointment and disillusionment are the end results.

♦ Questioning can place full responsibility for problem solving on you. Colleagues are left with the impression that they are only a bystander in the process. Remember that it is impossible to get anyone to have ownership of the problem and commitment to a plan without his or her involvement.

♦ People become dependent and rightfully lazy when they are not actively involved in both identifying the problem and finding solutions. This situation is not unlike the problem of learned helplessness found in many students, that is, students have learned over time that they are incapable of solving their own problems and as a result feel helpless.

♦ The process of questioning is inefficient. Consultees often know better what direction the conversation should move than do you. They have had more experience with the problem and they were responsible for raising the initial question.

♦ Inaccurate information may be provided. There are several reasons why this might happen. Consultees may respond only superficially when pressed, tell you what you seem to want to hear rather than what is true, and fabricate information in order to protect themselves if trust is absent.

♦ Resentment is created when questions are asked out of curiosity, rather than when they have a direct bearing on the problem. It is rare that more than a dozen relevant questions can be generated about anything.

Questions are a benchmark of the degree to which you are actively listening. The greater the number of questions, the less likely it is that you are using active listening skills such as paraphrasing and reflecting.

Why not use why questions?

Why questions should be used sparingly. In our culture, the word *why* can denote disapproval, displeasure, and judgment by a superior being. Many people perceive a why question as a set up for blame and condemnation leaving them no recourse but to defend themselves, counterattack, or avoid and escape the entire situation. Imagine how you might respond to these questions:

♦ "Why do you think that?"
♦ "Why do you feel that way?"

When why questions are used, they should focus primarily on securing information and ideas, rather than on feelings and emotions. Why questions, such as the following, can be used to explore relevant, factual information:

♦ "Why would this idea work?"
♦ "Why do you think students are behaving this way?"
♦ "Why do you think you feel the way you do?"

Because why questions can be so personal, this same data could be acquired by using the why question in a slightly different way:

♦ "Sam is behaving in X manner. Have any ideas why?"
♦ "You seem to feel . . . . Can you pinpoint why?"

In a nonthreatening atmosphere where trust and respect are established and the voice tone is appropriate, more risks can be taken using why questions such as these:

♦ "Why are you using this particular strategy?"
♦ "Marta did not show up today during her scheduled time. Why?"
♦ "Why is Sammy failing?"

Having said that why questions can be employed under ideal conditions, it still is wise to proceed with a great deal of caution. It makes no sense to risk losing the trust and confidence you have worked so hard to establish.

USING I-MESSAGES

When colleagues or friends are experiencing a problem, active listening is required. You are their sounding board; you facilitate their ability to find solutions to their problems. However, there are those difficult times in everyone's life when you must tell people that their behavior is unacceptable or is creating a problem for you. At such times, it is necessary to be assertive and to confront them so that a possible solution can be negotiated for your problem.

It is unfortunate that many people equate confrontation with an aggressive, noncaring, destructive act, typically used to hurt others. If the intention is to hurt people, it is not confronting, but attacking.

Be careful when confronting others to select the appropriate language so that people can listen and can continue to listen to the message that you are trying to send. Language that communicates ownership of the problem, makes a plea for help, and is not attacking can be achieved best through I-messages (Gordon, 1977).

I-messages are sometimes called *leveling* because you are being straightforward, open, and honest about your feelings, how someone's behavior is affecting you, and what you need instead. I-messages have four basic components:

1. A brief description of the behavior that is unacceptable to you or causing you stress.

2. The concrete effects or outcomes of that behavior on you personally.

3. Your true feelings about the person's behavior.

4. A description of the behavior that is preferred.

If you are not already in the habit of sending I-messages, you will find that they require contemplation and time to construct. Let us look more specifically at each component. First, you must describe exactly what the person is doing to cause you stress:

◆ "When feedback is offered that I did not request . . . ."
◆ "When our work-related problems are discussed with colleagues before they are discussed with me . . . ."

Second, you must describe how their behavior affects you. In other words, what is the skin off your nose?

◆ "I cannot listen effectively."
◆ "I lose the trust that I need to have for us to continue to work collaboratively."

Third, you must describe your true feelings if you want I-messages to have the power to grab people's attention. It is often very difficult for people to either identify their feelings or put a label on them. Check your solar plexus; what emotion is festering? What would you call it?

◆ "I feel devalued . . . ."
◆ "I am disappointed . . . ."
◆ "I feel distressed . . . ."
◆ "I am concerned . . . ."

It is not expressing an emotion to state:

◆ "I feel that our effectiveness is jeopardized . . . ."
◆ "I feel that people should work cooperatively . . . ."

These are thinking statements camouflaged under the word "feel."

Fourth, you must describe the behavior that you really want instead of the one you got. You need to explicitly state what you need and not leave it up to chance or wait for someone to guess what it is that will make you happy. Frequently this component is neglected, yet we know that it is unlikely that people will be able to read our minds. Positive examples of this element include:

◆ "What I need is for you to ask me questions so that I figure out what I need to change."
◆ "What I need is for you to discuss our issues with me."

The examples above are I-messages that we may have to send to colleagues. As you can see, they are difficult to construct and even more difficult to send. The examples below are complete I-messages in which all four components are present:

◆ "I feel very discouraged when a plan that we both agreed on is not implemented, because my time and energy are wasted. What I need is some feedback on what happened to it."

◆ "I am disappointed that I was not notified when the program was not working to your satisfaction, because I feel jointly responsible for its success. In the future, I need to be included in decisions that affect both of us."

◆ (To an administrator) "When I am not involved in the decisions that affect my class, I feel hurt because I am devalued as a professional. I need to be notified in advance and have my opinion, at least, considered when making the final decision."

◆ "When I see that students we share are primarily on a punishment system, I feel sad because I see the debilitating side effects. I need for us to mutually design a positive system that meets both our needs."

Undoubtedly, none of these people will feel ecstatic about receiving these messages. Individuals rarely like to be told that their behavior is causing a problem for others, no matter how nicely it is worded. However, they are much more likely to reconsider and to modify their behavior than if they had been scolded, warned, blamed, put down, lectured, or talked down to, as is more commonly the practice when people use You-messages (see next section).

There is a basic structure that you can use to formulate your own I-messages. Consider taking some time right now to write at least one I-message to the person who is probably on your mind as you read this:

- ◆ "I feel . . . when [describe behavior] . . . because [how it affects you] . . . ."
- ◆ "What I need is . . . ."

When you are beginning to learn how to send I-messages, it is not unusual to feel awkward, self-conscious, and afraid that people will perceive you as insincere. This is to be expected. Learning new communication skills is similar to learning any new skill, whether that be a new language, skiing for the first time, or working with challenging colleagues. With practice, however, I-messages become more natural sounding and require less forethought.

People pay a heavy price emotionally if they do not learn how to send I-messages during the early stages of conflict, before a candle flame develops into a blazing inferno. Without this skill, people hesitate to confront others about their unacceptable behavior for fear of provoking resistance, evoking retaliation, and damaging the current or future relationship. The truth is that if you do not sent I-messages, it is just a matter of time before the relationship is damaged anyway. When we are passive and fail to get our needs met, we are likely to develop feelings of resentment, stress, and feelings of being constantly victimized by others.

When a person's behavior is interfering with you getting your needs met, you own the problem. The issue of problem ownership is crucial to the concept of I-messages. Too often, there is a tendency to blame others when our needs are not being met. This, obviously, is incorrect. It is our responsibility to get our needs met, not someone else's responsibility to do so. They have the right to meet their needs by doing the very thing that is causing us stress; it is our problem to solve. Make every effort to avoid getting angry with them as a person. You are perfectly justified, however, in being upset with their behavior and with the fact that you are not getting your needs met. That is normal.

To review, an I-message is a potent tool for the following four reasons:

1. It communicates ownership of the problem.

2. It makes an appeal to others for help in finding a solution.

3. It avoids making people defensive because you are not attacking them, only the problem.

4. It helps people understand what you really want from them.

I-messages do not indicate that people must change or how they should change. They are simply an honest appeal for help. It is probably these qualities that account for the amazing potency of I-messages (Gordon, 1977).

Sending an I-message in an attempt to influence others to change their behavior is only the first step in trying to solve the problem. After it has been delivered, it is necessary to switch back to active listening wherein you clearly express an attitude of empathy for the person's situation and an acceptance of him or her as an individual. Again, acceptance does not mean that you agree with the behavior that is interfering with you getting your needs met.

Shifting from talking to listening is fundamental to confrontation situations. People generally feel that if you are nice enough to listen to them express their needs, pressures, and feelings, they should be equally accommodating by listening to yours. In other words, if you listen from their point of view, they are more likely to listen from your point of view. In addition, listening empathically has the potential for dissipating anger, hurt, or embarrassment that may inhibit future collaboration.

After you have actively listened from their point of view, it is sometimes necessary to repeat your original I-message, or at least a modified version of it. Restating it reminds the other person that you, too, are a warm-blooded, caring human being who gets problems, has feelings, bleeds internally, and anguishes just like them.

If you feel reluctant to deliver an I-message, remember that you are not alone. No one enjoys sending or receiving an I-message. You always run the risk (as most subconsciously fear) that people may not like you, at least for the moment. If you currently are in the habit of sending I-messages, congratulate yourself since it does take a great deal of courage to assert yourself and confront others in a positive way.

USING YOU-MESSAGES

You-messages are very popular in our culture, but they are totally ineffective because they contain language that sounds abrasive, judgmental, condescending, or injurious to the self-esteem of the person confronted. They also can sound threatening, sarcastic, and moralistic (Gordon, 1977). The following You-messages may sound familiar to you:

+ "You do not involve me in decisions that . . . ."
+ "It makes no sense when you . . . ."
+ "I feel angry when you do not follow through."
+ "You did not answer my question."
+ "You misunderstood my statement."

Here are a few others that may put someone on the defensive:

+ "Surely you do not expect all students to learn at the same rate or in the same style."

+ "You need to design an individualized program if you expect Lori to behave appropriately in class."

+ "Why did you ask Gary questions? Did you not anticipate that he would not be able to answer them? You only embarrass him in front of his peers."

♦ "Here is what you ought to do. Require Ali to compute only half the questions for homework."

Gordon (1977) indicates that You-messages are never well received because:

♦ They make people feel guilty.
♦ They can be interpreted as blame, put-downs, criticism, and rejections.
♦ They communicate a lack of respect for others.
♦ They often cause reactive or retaliatory behavior.
♦ They damage the recipient's self-esteem.
♦ They cause resistance rather than openness to change.
♦ They can make a person feel hurt, and later, resentful.
♦ They often are perceived as punitive.

With this amount of destruction, only those who are unaware of their debilitating effects would continue to use them.

You-messages contain two major obstacles that severely inhibit communication and problem solving. First, people do not like to be told what to do or what not to do. They prefer to self-initiate change when it becomes apparent that their behavior is not productive for them. Secondly, when the finger of blame is pointed at a person, it communicates that he or she is responsible and therefore should feel guilty and awful. Establishing guilt, fault, and blame serves absolutely no purpose, yet we seem to be willing to commit valuable hours to finding the guilty parties and punishing them before we initiate problem solving.

It helps to remember that people do things for their reasons, to meet their needs, not to deliberately hurt us or annoy us, as we often mistakenly tell ourselves.

The most distinguishing feature of You-messages is that they do not accomplish your mission. Your intent was simply to request a change in behavior, but your words caused resistance, guilt, and resentment. This leaves you farther away from achieving your goal. Try using I-messages—they can change your life!

The Message

Communication, both listening and speaking, is an integral part of collaborative planning and problem solving. Unless you can express yourself in a clear and effective manner, little change is likely to occur. By learning to use questions appropriately and by communicating effectively through I-messages, you can develop trust, clarify mutual goals, share information, plan strategies, collaboratively problem solve, and spark people's creativity and enthusiasm. Why not give it a whirl? What can you lose?

6

WITH KNOWLEDGE COMES POWER. WITH SELF-KNOWLEDGE COMES FREEDOM—THE FREEDOM TO CHOOSE.

MY INTERPERSONAL STYLE

What are my strengths?
What are my liabilities?

What is one subject that never bores you? Who do you most enjoy learning about? A subject that is guaranteed to capture the attention of all of us is ourselves. We are often our favorite subject. We love to learn more about what makes us so good at what we do and how we can get in our own way at times, perhaps without even realizing it. Therefore, this chapter is dedicated totally to you as a unique human being.

Your uniqueness is, in part, defined by your interpersonal style. Your style communicates how you work with people and how you think about your world. In many ways, it reveals who you are. It is an expression of your essence and is as unique to you as your signature and fingerprints. Your style attracts some people, fascinates others, and unfortunately, irritates and repels others. Your style impacts everyone with whom you come in contact in your daily life, at home and at work. Learning about your unique style can not only help you to be a better co-worker, but it can enrich your life and launch you toward becoming the best of what you are capable of being.

WHY SHOULD YOU LEARN ABOUT YOUR STYLE?

Not surprisingly, the more you know about yourself, the more benefits you can realize. Self-knowledge has the potential for allowing you to:

- Identify your strengths and emotional needs.

- Understand why you do what you do. In other words, what motivates you, what drives you?

- Develop a higher level of self-confidence and self-worth.

- Understand why you are successful in some situations and fail miserably in others.

- Identify the blind spots that cause most of your interpersonal problems.

- Gain insights on how to use your personal strengths more creatively and productively.

- Become a more adaptable and versatile problem solver.

- Develop an awareness of how your style may positively or negatively affect others.

- Identify and minimize potential conflicts with others.

- Reduce stress by allowing you to be in control of yourself.

- Experience an overwhelming sense of freedom—freedom to accept yourself as a fully functioning human being with needs and limitations.

- Accept others as fully functioning human beings with needs and limitations.

With these potential benefits, it is clearly in your best interests to find out everything you can about your interpersonal style.

WHAT ARE INTERPERSONAL STYLES?

Styles can be viewed as particular ways of behaving—the way you socially interact, gather information, make decisions, achieve your goals, and meet your emotional needs. We all have behavioral preferences, that is, a preference for how we say and do things (Merrill & Reid, 1981). For example, when some people are making a decision, they only want to hear "the facts, ma'am, only the facts." Others only want to hear how people feel about the facts, while others are interested only in the inferences people make about the facts. Some people like to joke around at meetings, while others see this light banter as an interruption. Some people like to live on the edge, while others need some guarantees in life before they take risks. Many differences abound. It is a wonder that we get along as well as we do!

Personal needs, sometimes referred to as emotional hungers, heavily influence a person's style. Emotional hungers drive us. While it is true that we all have similar needs (Maslow, 1970), it is also true that individuals differ in terms of their most driving needs. For example, some people have high needs for attention. It would truly ruin their day if they walked through a room full of people and no one noticed them. For others, it would ruin their day if they walked through the same room and anyone noticed them. Some people like to work collaboratively on projects, while others prefer that the work be divided up so they can take it to their area and work alone. Some people prefer sports that involve the collective skills of everyone in order to win (e.g., hockey, basketball, soccer), while others prefer sports that can be done alone (e.g., figure skating, skiing, in-line skating). If you recognize these differences in behavior, you are well on the way to identifying interpersonal styles—yours, as well as those with whom you work and play, because behavior usually reflects emotional needs.

Complex human behaviors that make up people's styles have been identified and classified for years by psychologists, psychiatrists, sociologists, behavioral scientists, and others who are interested in the study of human behavior. Although no one likes to be classified and categorized, it is sometimes necessary to do so, especially in the initial stages when you want to get a relatively quick, and reasonably accurate, picture of how people are likely to behave when you work or play with them. If you can recognize people's styles, as well as your own, you are more likely to influence them in a positive way.

Extensive and innovative studies by several behavioral scientists have provided interesting models for observing, interpreting, and predicting human behavior. As a result of thirty years of field-based observations as well as a synthesis of a large number of studies, I have identified four distinct interpersonal styles. While one is apprehensive about labeling people for fear of stereotyping them into categories for life, for our purposes, we will label people as Achievers, Persuaders, Supporters, and Analysts. Figure 1 graphically symbolizes these four different styles. The models that follow help provide a conceptual bases for understanding the similarities and differences across styles.

FIGURE 1

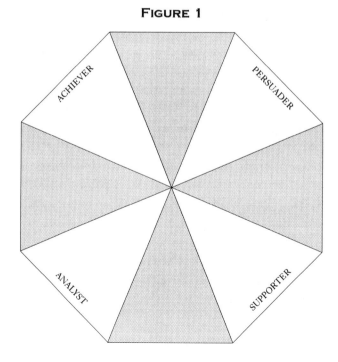

These four categories for explaining human behavior have been validated repeatedly by my experiences observing, questioning, listening to, and evaluating how people behave and influence their world in order to achieve their goals and meet their emotional needs.

DIMENSIONS OF HUMAN BEHAVIOR

Behavioral scientists suggest that there are several major dimensions that divide people into distinct learning and thinking styles. These polar opposites include:

- ◆ Concrete vs. Abstract
- ◆ Sequential vs. Random
- ◆ Active vs. Reflective
- ◆ Thinking vs. Intuitive
- ◆ Analyzer vs. Synthesizer
- ◆ Initiator vs. Responder

The two major dimensions that interact to create the four styles in this book are:

- ◆ Risk-Taking
- ◆ People Oriented

Risk-taking can be viewed along a continuum from high risk-taking behavior to low risk-taking behavior. Likewise, people oriented can range from being more people oriented to being less people oriented. Individuals who are high risk-takers behave differently from low risk-takers. Individuals who are more people oriented behave differently from those who are less people oriented.

High risk-takers can be characterized in a number of ways. Typically, they are people who jump in early no matter what the situation. They jump in early during conversations; they jump in early on projects. They are perceived by colleagues as being assertive and directive in nature. Colleagues also describe them as having a take charge attitude. (It is risky business to get out in front and lead a parade, especially when you do not know who is in it!) They hold strong opinions. (It is risky to stick with your opinion in spite of conflicting evidence.) They are often described as dreamers or creators. These high risk-takers do not hesitate to take the initiative in social situations. They have little difficulty making broad-brush statements about issues and people. A distinguishing characteristic is their ability and need to influence or control the thoughts and behaviors of others.

Individuals who are lower risk-takers are just the opposite. They scope out their environment before they jump in. They are more reserved, more calculated. They are the doers of the world; they are always around to make sure things get done. You can count on them. In social situations, they wait for people to approach them. They are more likely to ask questions than to make statements about issues and people. Their distinguishing characteristic is their lack of interest or effort to influence or control the thoughts and behaviors of others.

People-oriented behavior can be viewed as a continuum as well. At one end are individuals who seems to enjoy interacting with others. They love to collaborate with colleagues on projects and ideas. They are described by colleagues as being open, warm, approachable, responsive, informal, dramatic, flexible, emotional, and friendly. People-oriented individuals are thought to be easy to read because they readily display their emotions.

At the other end of the continuum are individuals who seem to prefer working alone. They are described by colleagues as being more solitary minded, more formal, less self-disclosing, more fact-based, and less personal. These people are less interested in what people are thinking and feeling and prefer that colleagues control or hide displays of emotions when interacting with them.

Differences in interpersonal styles are a function of the interaction between the two dimensions of risk-taking and people-orientation. Figure 2 illustrates that Achievers and Persuaders are higher risk-takers, while Supporters and Analysts are usually lower risk-takers. On the other hand, Figure 3 illustrates that Persuaders and Supporters generally are very people oriented, whereas Achievers and Analysts are likely to want to either work alone or have limited involvement with colleagues.

FIGURE 2

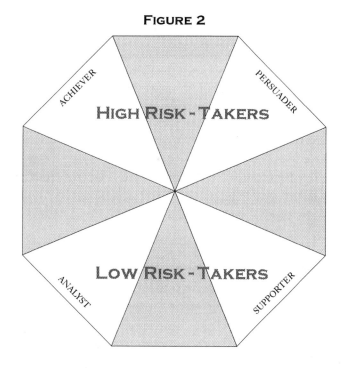

FIGURE 3

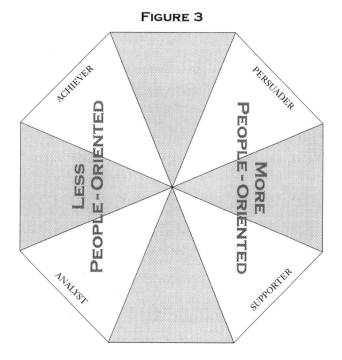

How are the Four Styles Different?

Each style has its own set of behaviors. Each has its strengths, liabilities, fears, stressors, and emotional needs. Each style has a repertoire of unique strategies it employs when working with colleagues and getting things done.

As you read through the following information that explains how to differentiate among the four interpersonal styles, please remember that all styles are excellent. No one style is better than another. The best style is the one that works for you.

Achievers

Achievers have been described using labels like chargers, drivers, initiators, developers, dominators, and tough battlers. They are easily recognized by their strong egos and their need to control situations in which they find themselves. They thrive on competitive situations, especially those that provide them with new and difficult challenges. They are very result oriented. They love jobs that will yield them positions of power, status, and prestige. Because they are self-confident, self-reliant, and accountability oriented, Achievers prefer to run projects themselves. They have difficulty delegating assignments unless they can be assured that the job will get done the best way—their way. Individuals with other styles believe that Achievers are too controlling at times.

When communicating, Achievers are forceful and direct. They do not hesitate to say exactly what is on their minds and, as a result, appear to lack empathy or sensitivity. They can listen intently if the subject has particularly significance for them, but they do not listen long. Whenever you interact with them, be brief and say it fast. Achievers appreciate colleagues who are equally straightforward and direct. Oblique discussions either irritate them or totally escape them.

As a general rule, do not worry about their feelings when communicating with them. In fact, if you stop and ask them how they feel, they are apt to respond with, "What feelings?" (One CEO of a Chicago-based company said very adamantly in an interview with the author, "I do not feel, I think!") This is not to suggest that they do not have feelings, they just do not consider them as important as facts and information. Unlike some other styles, they do not focus on feelings, their own or others. When you compliment them for any reason, they are apt to communicate a message (nonverbally, of course) that says, in essence, "Good! That makes two of us who admire the same person!"

Achievers' strengths and value to the group include:

♦ They are excellent problem solvers and decision makers. They are not afraid to make a decision even if it may prove to be wrong. They are quick to act and can be counted on to make things happen.

♦ They make good leaders because they are creative thinkers, encourage new ideas, and insist upon achieving objectives in an efficient manner.

The liabilities or qualities that can interfere with Achievers gaining the success they so rightly deserve include:

♦ They have a tendency to run over people in their efforts to get the job done efficiently and effectively.

♦ They lack caution in decision making and often are accused of taking a broad-brush approach.

♦ They are often impulsive in their efforts to get things done now.

Achievers use key phrases that can sometimes help identify their interpersonal style. For instance:

♦ "It is obvious to me . . . ."
♦ "Anyone can clearly see . . . ."
♦ "The fact of the matter is . . . ."
♦ "Who would not agree . . . ."

Their worst fear is losing control of people or events in their environment, especially in those circumstances for which they have been given authority. Under stress Achievers can become very agitated and impatient.

Persuaders

Persuaders have been described with labels such as influencers, promoters, social specialists, politicians, salespersons, and communicators. They are quickly recognizable by their intensely enthusiastic, optimistic, and fun loving approach to all situations. Persuaders love working with people on exciting challenges as long as the assignment has variety, mobility, freedom, and a great deal of personal recognition for their imaginative efforts. Persuaders are both futuristic and achievement oriented. They have an intuitive sense about how things should be, and they take the necessary risks to see their dreams through to completion.

The Persuaders' specialty is getting the job done in a friendly way. They are outgoing, articulate, and flexible. They possess a special quality for allowing people to feel comfortable with them almost immediately. Persuaders also have the ability to get people to feel good about themselves. They do this by validating people's self-worth through constant recognition, encouragement, and positive comments. Because they are emotional individuals, Persuaders can be very dramatic, excitable, and gregarious.

Persuaders' strengths and contribution to a group include:

♦ They are excellent communicators. If you have an idea to promote, give it to a Persuader.

♦ They are superb at motivating the unmotivated. They actually enjoy stimulating and inspiring disengaged individuals.

♦ They enjoy working with people. As a result, people enjoy working with them largely because they are high-spirited and entertaining.

The liabilities or qualities that can interfere with Persuaders' gaining the success they so rightly deserve include:

♦ They need to manage their time better. They give too much of their time away to insignificant others and less important issues.

♦ They are an easy mark for those who specialize in taking advantage of others because they trust people almost unquestioningly.

♦ They can be oblique when confronting people; they fear hurting others if they say exactly what is on their minds (and there is usually quite a lot on their minds).

Persuaders use key phrases that can sometimes help identify their interpersonal style:

♦ "Most people would agree . . . ."
♦ "People I trust suggest . . . ."
♦ "An exciting approach would be . . . ."
♦ "My personal experience tells me . . . ."

Their worst fears are criticism and disapproval of them as individuals. Under stress Persuaders appear preoccupied and manifest this behaviorally by being hyperactive or fidgety.

Supporters

Supporters have been described using labels like counselors, idealists, friendly helpers, crusaders, and traditionalists. They are identified by their sincere interest and concern (at times, over concern) for the welfare of all people. They are extremely helpful and dependable. They can always be counted on to be available in times of trouble. Supporters have very high ideals and standards for themselves and everyone else. This can occasionally get in their way. They believe that anything that is worth doing should be done well, to perfection, if possible. Supporters strive for mutual agreements on issues because they dislike conflict and will avoid it at all costs.

Supporters seek a broad range of views and feedback on issues, people, and events prior to making decisions. Risk-taking is not their strong suit. They are especially interested in people's values and feelings on many issues. More than anything else, Supporters need to be appreciated by those around them—family, peers, colleagues, and bosses.

Supporters' strengths and contribution to a group include:

- They have the only style that can work well with all types of people, from the gutter fighter to the working dead.

- They can achieve remarkable consistency in any undertaking because they are able to concentrate.

- They are superb listeners. As a result, they are able to provide moral support to everyone.

- They provide an environment that is calm, cooperative, and predictable. They are patient with everyone.

The liabilities or qualities that can interfere with Supporters gaining the success they so rightly deserve include:

- They hate and resist too much change. Small amounts of change are tolerable. Change interferes with their needs for security.

- They have a tendency to be too possessive about objects and people.

- In spite of their sincere efforts to help, they can often annoy colleagues by appearing too nice, too hospitable, and too available.

Supporters use key phrases that can sometime help identify their interpersonal style:

- "It is my personal feeling that . . . ."
- "Do you feel that . . . ?"
- "People need to appreciate . . . ."

Their worst fear is loss of security. They need stability and predictability in their lives. Under stress Supporters give the appearance of looking hurt or pouting.

Analysts

Analysts have been described using labels like objective thinkers, practitioners, diplomats, perfectionists, precision specialists, and long-range planners. They distinguish themselves from the other styles by being serious, accurate, systematic, and detail oriented. Analysts value high standards and quality control. They are quiet, disciplined, unassuming people who appear unemotional when dealing with colleagues. They rarely take any social initiative. If you want to meet or speak with Analysts, you will have to take the initiative as they tend to stay guarded and cautious until they feel they can trust you or the situation.

Analysts thrive in environments that contain clearly defined procedures, rules, and regulations. They insist on order, logic, predictability, and consistency. Risk-taking is outside of their universe. Analysts weigh all alternatives before making a decision. Their need to be thorough can delay decisions indefinitely. This can prove to be a liability for them.

Analysts' strengths and contributions to a group include:

- ◆ They have highly developed critical abilities and are intuitive about the potential outcomes of projects or programs.

- ◆ They insist that conclusions be based on carefully analyzed data derived from solid research. Therefore, errors due to poor judgment and quick decisions are significantly decreased when they are at the helm.

- ◆ They are great long range planners with unique abilities to plan tasks systematically from beginning to end.

The liabilities or qualities that can interfere with Analysts gaining the success they so rightly deserve include:

- ◆ They have difficulty making decisions because they search endlessly for the one best way. They procrastinate until they have seen the whole picture, not just the big picture.

- ◆ They need constant reassurance that what they are doing is being done right. They have a tendency to be overly precise.

Analysts use key phrases that can sometime help identify their interpersonal cognitive style:

♦ "Logic would dictate . . . ."
♦ "It stands to reason . . . ."
♦ "What guarantees are there that . . . ?"

Their worst fear is criticism of their work. Under stress Analysts withdraw from people and the situation.

CAUTION: There are no pure styles

A troublesome tendency, once labels have been placed on people, is to believe that each person so labeled is identical to every other person with the same label. Not so! For purposes of discussion and clarity, styles are presented here as though they are pure styles, and not as real human beings with whom you interact daily. Figure 4 shows how you can expect to see similar behaviors across the styles because they share common dimensions. You can expect Achievers and Persuaders to be similar in their approach to solving life's problems because they are both risk-takers, but they differ in their interest in building and maintaining relationships. Achievers and Analysts are similar in their lack of interest and attention to people's feelings, but they are dissimilar in their ability to take professional and personal risks. Similarly, Supporters and Analysts are somewhat alike in that both are lower risk-takers, but they differ in their awareness and concern for human beings as individuals. Persuaders and Supporters are both very social and personable, but differ in their comfort level with taking risks.

FIGURE 4

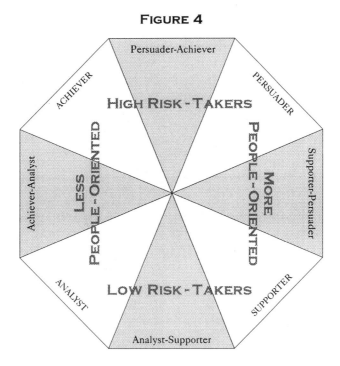

As you can see in the model, a person may use behaviors that lead you to believe that he or she is either a pure Achiever, a Persuader-Achiever, or an Achiever-Analyst. One can expect that a person with a Persuader-Achiever style would be more people oriented than a person who is primarily an Achiever, but less decisive in decision making. A person with an Achiever-Analyst style would be less risk-taking than the pure Achiever, but more precise in handling details, and so on, and so on! As a result of sharing common dimensions, eight fairly distinct styles are possible.

Styles that are directly opposite one another, that is, the Achiever and the Supporter or the Persuader and the Analyst, have the least in common. As a result, they have to work very hard to understand and tolerate each other. Because they share no common dimensions, they find it difficult to comprehend and accept how their opposite style feels or thinks. Each one, however, has qualities that their opposite styles must develop if they hope to work effectively with colleagues.

As you observe human behavior, you will notice that most people have a little of each style. It is likely that they have learned to use other behaviors for interacting in their efforts to achieve their goals and meet their emotional needs. Learning to adapt to one's environment in a flexible manner is an important human trait. Most individuals function daily in a very fluid manner. Even though people have one primary style, they are able to draw on secondary and tertiary styles. Figure 5 shows that the closer people are to the center, the more fluid and adaptable they are. Some people function so close to the center that it is difficult to recognize their style. They are chameleons: they can be whatever they need to be in order to enjoy success. On the other hand, some people function at the outside edges of their style and it is very easy to recognize their style; their behavior is consistent and predictable.

FIGURE 5

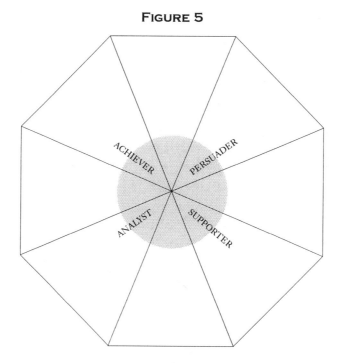

YOUR EXTREME STYLE

Figure 6 graphically symbolizes how individuals can operate outside their extreme style. These individuals definitely do not experience the flexibility and adaptability they need to work effectively with anyone. Too much of any good thing can cause problems. For example, your major strength may be that you are very intense—a seemingly positive attribute. However, intensity, taken to its extreme, can be intrusive and alienating. Similarly, your strength may be your ability to see all sides of a story. This can become a weakness when you are unable to make a decision because you do see all sides of the story.

FIGURE 6

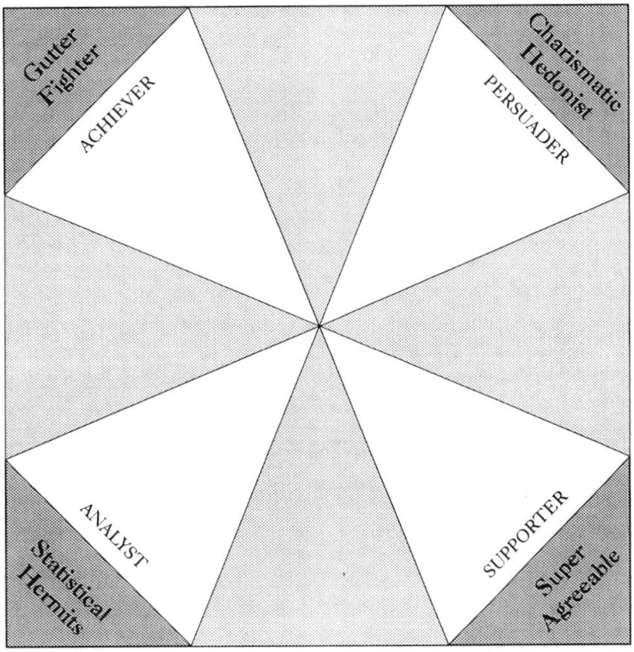

Achievers can be so high in risk-taking behavior and so in low people-oriented skills that they can be described or labeled by others as "gutter fighters." They are willing to do whatever it takes to survive. They should not be confused with pragmatists.

Persuaders with their charismatic qualities, can influence others to do things that may harm them. Some unethical preachers and politicians come to mind, but shall not be mentioned here. An extreme Persuader is the Charismatic Hedonist.

Supporters can be so sensitive to human needs and are such low risk-takers that they can become immobilized. Rather than risk disagreement, they are likely to give in to pressure, thereby earning the title Super Agreeables.

Analysts can be so obsessed with accuracy and the need to work independently that they can give the appearance of being Statistical Hermits.

YOUR PREDOMINANT STYLE

Everybody has a predominant style, a central tendency, and a preference for the way they approach people and situations. Even though people have a predominant style, they are unlikely to be clearly one style all the time. Human beings are not easily classified and have the potential for being very flexible and adaptable in various situations. It is interesting to note, however, that even though people have the potential for being flexible and adaptive, and that these abilities are necessary to survive, approximately 75-85% of the population find it extremely difficult to adapt easily. Old habits die hard because they have served people well in the past and are intermittently reinforced; consequently, people are extremely resistant to change.

Even though a person's style tends to remain stable over time and across situations, it also is true that some people and some situations can provoke them into an alien style. Have you known people who bring out the best in you and others who bring out the worst in you? It seems that when our emotional buttons are pushed in a negative way, we regress to strategies that seemed to work when we were previously confronted with conflict. Unfortunately, these old patterns of behavior used without much forethought only compound the problem. To avoid a miserable experience for everyone, try to identify those people and situations that bring out your best qualities.

Your style can vary somewhat as a function of many things:

- The situation you are in.
- The people you are with.
- Your needs at the moment.
- Your objectives in a particular situation.
- Your experiences working in groups.
- Your current stress levels.

Everybody should rejoice in their own style, because all styles can create greatness. There is no one best style. All styles can be good. The best style for you is the one that serves your purposes, meets your needs, and is situationally appropriate.

WHERE DOES YOUR STYLE COME FROM?

Each person is a product of many influences in his or her lifetime. Here are a few of them:

- Emotional needs can affect how you perceive your environment and how you work with people.

- Economic needs can affect how much risk you are willing to take to influence change.

- Past and current role models can affect how you behave.

- Mentors who spent time interacting with you and questioning your beliefs, assumptions, attitudes, and values can affect how you now function.

- Values that you hold can affect how you make decisions.

- Heredity has provided you with a propensity for being who you are.

- Experiences, both successes and failures, can influence how you now manage your life.

- Training and education have provided you with a forum for questioning old attitudes and ways of behaving.

Styles for behaving often are unconscious and, as a result, have a tendency to repeat themselves again and again to the extent that it makes it possible for them to be brought to our conscious level. It is this awareness that allows people to assess and alter their individual styles if they so choose.

HOW CAN YOU DETERMINE YOUR STYLE?

Several options are available for you to assess your style. A good way to start this self-assessment is to spend some quiet time soul searching, during which you ask yourself the following questions:

- ◆ What are my goals in life?
- ◆ What are my values? What do I hold near and dear?
- ◆ What are my most powerful needs?
- ◆ What are my worst fears?
- ◆ What motivates me?
- ◆ What are my timelines for meeting my most pressing needs?
- ◆ What am I prepared to do to meet my needs?
- ◆ What strategies have I used in the past to influence others?
- ◆ What immobilizes me?
- ◆ How would I survive if my worst fears came true?
- ◆ How much of a risk-taker am I?
- ◆ What role do people play in satisfying my needs?

Other self-revealing questions include:

- ◆ How would my friends or peers describe me?
- ◆ What are the qualities I like in the people with whom I work? Why?
- ◆ How do I spend my free time? Why?
- ◆ Does my free time include or exclude people? Why?
- ◆ What kind of pictures do I display on my walls and what might they reveal?

If you take time to examine these areas, the results can yield a great deal of knowledge about your style. Look for patterns and tendencies, then compare your findings with the information provided on the four basic styles presented earlier in this chapter.

A second option for assessing your style is to interview family members, friends, or peers. Ask them to describe you. Use many of the same questions you would ask yourself. Use these people only as facilitators for self-examination. Do not embrace without question their descriptions of you. Meticulously edit each statement. Have faith that you probably know yourself better than anyone.

A third alternative for assessing your personal style is to use one of several self-assessment inventories that are commercially available, such as the *Interpersonal Style Questionnaire* by Anita DeBoer (see Appendix D). Even though many of these instruments have been empirically researched for a number of years across various populations, it is important to remember that any such tool does not provide a complete and absolute picture of you. You are much more complex than this. These instruments merely provide a structure that focuses attention on aspects of yourself that you may not have previously identified. They can also allow you to focus on aspects of yourself that you were not fully aware of—your hidden self. Always feel comfortable editing and rejecting information you feel does not describe you accurately. Remember, it is only a test created by humans such as yourself.

KEY SKILLS FOR SELF-IMPROVEMENT

No one is perfect, so do not waste your valuable energy wishing you were significantly different. You are what you are and you are not likely to change your basic style significantly. Yet, you can overcome some of your weaknesses once they are identified if you have a desire to do so. Should you decide to change some behaviors, it helps to concentrate on improving just one key skill at a time. Here are a few skills to consider:

◆ *Achievers* could expend some energy on one of the following:

- Listen more attentively to the ideas of others.
- Develop more empathy for the feelings of others.
- Involve people more actively in decision making.
- Take more time to study situations and people before making decisions.

- ♦ *Persuaders* could expend some energy on one of the following:
  - Pay closer attention to details.
  - Double check information that is given and received.
  - Manage time more efficiently.
  - Do not lose sight of goals.
  - Learn to control emotions in some situations.

- ♦ *Supporters* could expend some energy on one of the following:
  - Learn to take risks.
  - Take more initiative to achieve personal goals.
  - Develop more firmness and directness on issues of importance.
  - Communicate a shared responsibility for students. In other words, stop saying, "*My* kids."

- ♦ *Analysts* could expend some energy on one of the following:
  - Learn to make decisions more efficiently by taking calculated risks.
  - Increase interest in and awareness of people's feelings.
  - Learn to take the initiative in problem-solving situations and meeting new people.
  - Learn to be more comfortable working collaboratively.

STRATEGIES UNIQUE TO EACH STYLE

Each interpersonal style employs a distinct and somewhat unique set of strategies for working with people, managing problems, and making decisions. Think about your own style and try to identify the strategies that you currently use. Strategies include:

- ♦ *Achievers*, for the most part, employ strategies that are results oriented, efficient, forceful, direct, independent, and impersonal. They have a tendency to try to control both the events and people in problem-solving situations.

- ♦ *Persuaders*, for the most part, employ strategies that stimulate, inspire, and excite people to action. They include people in decision-making because they believe that involvement and ownership in decisions is important. They do business in a friendly way while pushing forward to achieve their objectives.

◆ *Supporters*, for the most part, employ strategies that have proven effective in the past, have been around for a long time, and are familiar to everyone. They place heavy emphasis on working with and for people, while making frequent references to feelings, friends, and family. One of their key strategies is to ask open and indirect questions, thereby influencing others through listening.

◆ *Analysts*, for the most part, employ strategies that are organized, preplanned, logical, researched, and relatively impersonal. They pay a great deal of attention to small details that are generally ignored by the other styles, but are essential to systematic and smooth operations. They combine mounds of factual information in an intuitive way as they move toward decisions.

TIMELINES FOR GOAL ACHIEVEMENT

All styles are goal directed, but each style follows a different path to success. All approaches are effective if they achieve the goals and meet people's emotional needs. What often sets the styles apart and causes major conflict at times is the timelines they set for achieving the goals. Achievers and Persuaders want to get the job done now, while Supporters and Analysts view fast paced change with a great deal of trepidation and skepticism. However, by the time each style works through its fears and/or any resistance they may have created, they are all likely to get the real job done at about the same time as Achievers and Persuaders.

To elaborate on the idea of timelines and change, imagine being involved with each of the four styles as they design a five-year plan for change. The likely outcomes involving each style include:

◆ *Achievers* would have a plan in place in six months, but by the time they worked through all of the resistance and sabotage from the people affected by the change, the plan might not be operational or running smoothly for at least five years.

◆ *Persuaders* would need about a year to sell the plan to all but a few hard core resisters. During the second or third year, however, some general resistance would surface when those affected by the plan realized that they had been oversold on its benefits. The plan could be operational by the fifth year when everyone was comfortable with his or her new role.

◆ *Supporters* would move very slowly toward the goal by first determining if there is a real need for change and then allocate sufficient time to get people ready for it. Everyone's emotions and needs would be addressed. After a consensus was reached on how to proceed, everyone would be expected to support the group decision. At the end of five years, the plan would finally be in place with everyone relatively content.

◆ *Analysts* would need at least four and a half years to fully research the benefits and liabilities of any change. They would use most of the time to design a carefully organized, systematic process for implementing the plan. Flowcharts would be their bible for approaching people and informing them of their new responsibilities. As with the other styles, at the end of five years, a plan would be in place with everything clearly spelled out.

STYLES AND PROFESSIONAL GROUPS

Although there is no one best style, it is possible that some styles are more appropriate for some professions than are others. It may also be true that individuals with certain styles are drawn to some professions more than others because of the opportunities for success. Success is defined as meeting one's emotional needs. Styles and their typical professional affiliations include:

◆ *Achievers* prefer administrative or executive positions where they have more power and control. They like positions that do not require them to work collaboratively with people on a full-time basis. They are drawn to positions like presidents of organizations, efficiency experts, political advisors, administrators, or any position that requires an up front or a behind-the-scenes, high achieving individual.

◆ *Persuaders* tend to be politicians, actors, TV hosts, salespeople, consultants, or seminar leaders. Those who need recognition and applause are likely to have Persuader styles.

◆ *Supporters* prefer professions that are altruistic. A high number of nurses, teachers, social workers, and other helping professionals manifest Supporter styles. Their primary concern is the welfare of people.

◆ *Analysts* are drawn to professions such as architecture, accounting, computer programming, mathematics, or research sciences. It is refreshing to know that airline pilots are usually Analysts. This style is very detail oriented and has no need to be socializing with passengers in the cabin of the plane, as you might find with a Persuader style.

Even though certain styles are attracted to some professions more than others, you can also find all four styles within a particular profession. Think about people you know in the medical profession. Achievers are likely to be attracted to the role of a surgeon (with its need for limited bedside manners); Persuaders are likely to show up on television shows where they can discuss and market good health; Supporters are likely to be our family doctors; and Analysts are likely to be at university hospitals doing research on rare diseases.

Most professions require integrated styles. To be successful, people need a bit of each style, or they need to be flexible enough to shift to more appropriate strategies when necessary. For example, trial lawyers need to be bold, confident, determined Achievers but they need to switch to dramatic, articulate, emotional Persuaders when they are presenting to a jury. At times, they may need to use a Supporter style when they have to make an impassioned plea for the rights of the underprivileged or the less fortunate if they wish to influence the jury's decision. It also would be essential, prior to the trial, that they be intuitive, thorough, accurate, detail-oriented Analysts who spent sufficient time studying the precise facts of the case. Teaching requires many of the same skills that an excellent trial attorney possesses.

DEFENSIVE BEHAVIORS

People are needs driven and therefore work diligently to get their needs met to increase or maintain their self-esteem. However, under stressful conditions where emotional needs have not been met for an extended period of time, each interpersonal style can regress to style specific, defensive behaviors:

♦ *Achievers*, when under pressure, can be extremely dominating and will attempt to control others by intimidating them with a louder voice and proximity control. They make controlling statements like, "Any fool can see . . . ," or "It is clearly evident to most people . . . ."

♦ *Persuaders*, when under pressure, can be verbally aggressive and will attempt to control others with emotional outbursts that contain negative and accusing statements like, "Why do you always . . . !"

♦ *Supporters*, when under pressure, can be very conforming and will acquiesce to whatever demands are placed on them. In other words, they give up and give in, at least on the surface. They overuse, "I am sorry. I did not mean to . . . ."

♦ *Analysts*, when under pressure and their needs are not being met, are experts at avoiding and escaping people and situations. They race out of these stressful situations with a simple, "Excuse me," and disappear.

All styles have the potential for employing any one of these defensive tactics under high stress conditions. It depends upon the individual, the people with whom they are working, and the situation with which they are faced. Prior success using these defensive tactics, can also influence which defensive strategy a person might use. Any defensive behavior that was reinforced previously because it worked will be used more frequently in the future. Behaviors over time become habits.

Defensive behavior is a normal and necessary response to tension and should be viewed as such. Whenever you feel your emotional garbage bucket is full, it is normal to want to dump it, hopefully not on others, but you need to dump it somewhere. Mental health experts commonly argue that people who never express their angry feelings are sick, while those who do, are healthy. (They are friendless, divorced, unemployed, but healthy!) The trick is to find the balance by recognizing the appropriate time and place for expressing anger. Dumping your anger indiscriminately can cause defensiveness in people. This can negatively impact effective communication and collaborative problem solving. As we all know, when trust is reduced or broken, and it is very difficult to increase or reestablish it.

Responsible, Win/Win behavior is the key. You need to meet your needs and do it in a way that others can meet their needs as well. One cannot be done at the expense of the other, or all is lost. Win/Win solutions are necessary if change is to be effective and long lasting.

THE MESSAGE

What makes consulting interesting and challenging is the diversity of people with whom we work. We all have different strengths, liabilities, fears, and stresses. Fortunately, there is no one best style. We can all develop the best of our own unique style so that it works for us. The key to working and communicating effectively with colleagues is recognizing and acknowledging style differences.

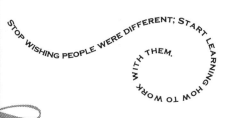

THEIR INTER-PERSONAL STYLE

What are their strengths?
What are their liabilities?

hink of people with whom you love to work. Knowing that you are going to see them makes your day. Why do you like to work with these people? What behaviors do they have that you respect? In case you have not noticed, we are talking about style. Now, think of people with whom you would not like to work if you had a choice. Knowing that you are going to see them puts a smudge on your day. Why would you just as soon avoid them? What behaviors do they have that you do not value? What behaviors irritate you? Again, we are talking about style. Have you ever been asked to work collaboratively with people that you do not really know? Has that ever caused you some anxiety? Are you concerned about how they will accept you? Are you concerned about how you will accept them? Would knowing more about style help?

The ability to predict your environment and the behavior of those with whom you interact is a necessary skill for physical and emotional survival. Brain studies indicate that emotional disturbance and pathology are developed from adverse events over which one has little control and little predictability. Identifying the interpersonal styles of people with whom you work and play can reduce stress. Only when you see how your style can mesh with theirs can you begin to achieve your goal for becoming a valuable co-worker: a person who uses Win/Win strategies.

An important quality of a successful person is flexibility. Flexibility requires, however, that you be aware of the dynamics of interpersonal styles. The moment you begin to pay attention to style, both yours and theirs, you begin the process of positively influencing others to effect change. You may be surprised, even shocked, at how you have been setting traps for yourself for years by using the wrong strategy in the wrong place at the wrong time with the wrong people. All that can change.

Every day you think about many things and make many decisions, sometimes independently, but more often than not, collaboratively. Whenever you are working with people, it helps to remember that everyone makes decisions and communicates in distinctly different ways. What causes conflict and inhibits problem solving is believing that your way of viewing the world is the only way, or equally destructive, the right way.

If you organize and predict people's behavior using the same four interpersonal styles described in the last chapter, the Achiever, the Persuader, the Supporter, and the Analyst, you can save yourself many headaches, and more importantly, create many more successes for yourself and your colleagues.

HOW TO RECOGNIZE THEIR STYLE

It is a fairly simple task to identify the predominant style of another person once you know what to look for. Behaviors tend to cluster together to form an interpersonal style. Everyone, whether they know it or not, flashes their essence from the moment they enter a room. What you are watching for are those key indicators or giveaway signals that enable you to recognize a person's style.

As you observe the behavior of people with whom you are unfamiliar, keep in mind that the first bits of information you put together to identify their style is only a beginning step. This initial information is likely to be incomplete and a little distorted because it is only your perceptions of them, not their perceptions of themselves. Mid-course corrections are always encouraged because sometimes people are not what you initially pegged them to be. Some people have spent a great deal of time, energy, and money developing an image (similar to our politicians) so that "what you sees is not what you gots!" As you learn more, you may have to change your assumptions and the way you work with them.

Styles can be predicted using several data sources:

- ◆ Observe the person's behavior.
- ◆ Observe the person's different environments.
- ◆ Talk with the person.
- ◆ Talk with the person's colleagues.

Observe behavior

Direct observation of a person's behavior is an excellent strategy for recognizing styles. However, when you observe behaviors you need to "see" as intently with your ears as you do with your eyes. It means paying close attention to verbal and nonverbal behavior in order to sense the subtle messages people are sending. It means watching to see if they listen, how well they listen, and how long they listen. It means noting their overall appearance, recurring phrases, idiosyncrasies, body language, facial expressions, voice qualities, and their comfort level with physical contact. Eye contact and hand shakes alone can yield a wealth of information about a person's style.

Observing behavior consists of more than merely monitoring and recording observable signals. It also involves an evaluation of what you are feeling as you observe and interact with people. Take time to acknowledge and evaluate this important information before you commit yourself to a plan for working together. Do not hesitate to trust your intuition. It is often loaded with valuable data selected and sorted by your subconscious mind and processed at a higher level than the simple facts you have collected. When you meet or observe someone, try to load your memory bank with a plethora of symbols that can signal that person's interpersonal style.

All the data you gather through astute observations must be meaningfully organized if you are going to predict a person's style. Are they a high risk-taking, less people-oriented Achiever? Are they a high risk-taking, more people-oriented Persuader? Are they a lower risk-taking, more people-oriented Supporter? Are they a lower risk-taking, less people-oriented Analyst? The following descriptors can help you in your quest. These descriptive behaviors are typical of each style, but are not always present.

ACHIEVERS

What are their behavioral descriptors?

- Determined
- Demanding
- Decisive
- Efficient
- Confident
- Forceful
- Dominating
- Impatient
- Egocentric
- Value accomplishment
- Short attention span
- Broad-brush approach
- Love difficult challenges
- Embrace change

What are their most driving needs?

- Power
- Authority
- Prestige
- Directness

PERSUADERS

What are their behavioral descriptors?

- Inspiring
- Optimistic

- Gregarious
- Stimulating
- Enthusiastic
- Articulate
- Emotional
- Impulsive
- Dramatic
- Value relationships
- Excitable
- Outgoing

What are their most driving needs?

- Recognition
- Popularity
- Acceptance
- Freedom

SUPPORTERS

What are their behavioral descriptors?

- Respectful
- Good listeners
- Noncommittal
- Dependable
- Conforming
- Willing
- Loyal
- Patient
- Steady
- Predictable
- Can work with anybody
- Values family

What are their most driving needs?

- Appreciation
- Job security
- Tradition
- Status quo

ANALYSTS

What are their behavioral descriptors?

- ♦ Industrious
- ♦ Accurate
- ♦ Persistent
- ♦ Detail oriented
- ♦ Serious
- ♦ Cautious
- ♦ Systematic
- ♦ Organized
- ♦ Indecisive
- ♦ Values quality
- ♦ Impersonal
- ♦ Thorough

What are their most driving needs?

- ♦ Order
- ♦ Reassurance
- ♦ Predictability
- ♦ Standard procedures

It is often difficult to pinpoint exactly which style someone is because some people have integrated the styles so masterfully that they can be whatever they need to be for the moment. They do it fluidly, with little effort, and with real sincerity.

Observe environments

A second major source of information regarding a person's style comes from closely observing his or her personal environment, either at home or at work. Note the arrangement of furniture in a room. Does it appear cold or intimate? Is the room cluttered or orderly? Note the types of pictures on the walls. Is the content family, pets, posters, motivational slogans, certificates, diplomas, or awards? If the wall hangings are pieces of art, what is the subject, color, size, and position in the room? Is humor involved? You are looking for a theme that would indicate a predominant style. If you are observing a person's work environment be cautious, it may reflect school policy or a administrator's preference rather than the individual's preferred style.

Talk with people

There is good reason to believe that the best way to find out about people is to talk to them. They are probably the best source of information on themselves. Be careful not to bombard anyone with a series of questions. Ask open ended, indirect questions, then listen. Useful starter questions include:

- How do you spend your free time? How does that please you?
- What are the things you like best and least about your work environment? Why?
- In what ways does your work meet your needs?
- How would your peers describe you?
- Would you prefer to lead a group or facilitate a group?
- What are the qualities you like in the people with whom you associate? Are they similar to you, or would they complement you?
- What subjects did you enjoy studying in school? What did you enjoy most about them?
- What are your past work experiences? How much pleasure did those jobs yield?
- How would your friends or peers describe you?
- Does your free time include or exclude people. Why?

Talk with colleagues

If it is either impossible or inappropriate to assess a person's style by talking with them directly, an alternative is to talk with people who know the person. The areas of information and the types of questions you use are identical, or at least very similar, to those you used when observing and interacting with the person directly.

When you have collected the information you need from observing their environment and interviewing them and their colleagues, reread the behavioral descriptors for each style and try to determine their predominant style. This information is critical if you want to know how to work successfully with them.

THE MIXING AND MESHING OF STYLES

Some styles attract one another forming an immediate bond, both personally and professionally. The chemistry is right. Their styles are mutually reinforcing, and the relationship lasts over time. Unfortunately, it is not always possible to predict which styles will mutually attract. It varies depending upon each person's needs at the time. Sometimes opposite styles will attract one another; at other times, identical styles will attract one another. It is likely that individuals with similar needs have the highest potential for developing productive relationships.

The chemistry between styles can be toxic as well. At times, two styles will mesh temporarily, then the situation turns sour, and the results are disastrous. At other times, just the presence of a certain style will trigger a negative reaction in you. You immediately get into a defensive stance. When this happens, it is perplexing and disturbing for everyone, especially you.

While you are working with people, ask yourself the following critical questions so that you can determine how your styles might mesh:

- ♦ What is my style?
- ♦ What is their style?
- ♦ How does their style normally affect me?
- ♦ How can my style affect them?
- ♦ How can I adapt my style so that the results are mutually beneficial?

For people to work cooperatively in groups, a balance of all styles or viewpoints is necessary within the group. Groups that contain a high incidence of only one style are likely to experience high conflict and low productivity. Imagine a group with nothing but Achievers! Can you see them constantly pushing, shoving, and jockeying for positions of power and control? As a result, little would get accomplished. What about Supporters? They are likely to be so concerned about how their peers are feeling about the issues that confront them, they become immobilized and unable to make any decisions. Analysts are likely to search endlessly for more data so that they can be sure they are making the right decision. And Persuaders? They would spend all their time communicating avidly and convincingly with one another about all the possibilities. As a result, little would get accomplished.

A well functioning group should have an Achiever, a Persuader, a Supporter, and an Analyst. The Achiever would lead the group and get them to focus on the task. The Persuader would make sure the group was motivated and having fun. The Supporter would make sure that the group used good communication skills (turn taking, clarifying, empathic listening). And the Analyst would make sure the group did their homework (research) before they made a decision to act. The message is clear: We need everybody for things to work smoothly. We need the unique strengths of each style.

VIGNETTES OF STYLES

The four interpersonal styles can be recognized and understood by observing how teachers, each with different styles, might be expected to organize and manage their classrooms. Each style is depicted through short vignettes. Again, a word of caution is necessary: Do not expect to observe pure styles in real life such as those portrayed here. Styles rarely exist in pure form. But do look for a theme that might identify a person's predominant style.

The Achiever

Ms. Achiever is a sixth-grade classroom teacher. As you read about how she does things, ask yourself, "Does she have a counterpart at my school?"

Ms. Achiever is very direct and forthright with her students. She says it like it is, quickly and briefly; whether they be classroom rules or directions for classroom activities. While her lessons emphasize specific facts to be recalled, she does offer many personal opinions on issues. She can appear dogmatic at times. She frequently uses short, pointed anecdotes or analogies to efficiently demonstrate a concept. She is gifted at cutting through large amounts of theory and objectively presenting the facts in a simplified manner.

Ms. Achiever is very results oriented. She uses daily quizzes and weekly tests to provide concrete evidence of learner outcomes. Accountability is a driving force in her life. Feedback to students on the quality of their work is delivered succinctly and directly.

Ms. Achiever likes to challenge her students with projects and activities and encourages them to develop new and innovative ideas. She is determined to get the best from her students by demanding quality and by insisting that assignments be submitted on time. She demonstrates a keen interest in her work and an intense, continuous striving for task accomplishment. This message is conveyed clearly to her students.

Ms. Achiever prefers to use a direct-instruction approach when teaching and delivers her content very well this way. When she directs questions to students, responses are expected to be immediate and brief. She gets impatient when her students do not manage their time well and produce less than quality results.

Students respect Ms. Achiever but avoid approaching her unless there is a real need for her assistance. Shy students feel intimidated by her seemingly curt remarks. In addition, Ms. Achiever's classroom often is described by parents and peers as being somewhat cold or impersonal, but she is considered to be an excellent teacher by everyone. Bulletin boards are filled with current events, scientific facts, and important historical events. Her reputation for appearing uncaring and lacking empathy probably results from episodes in which students had complained about or had struggled through difficult tasks. Her typical responses to these situations were, "Do not feel sorry for yourself! You will be fine," or "I told you you could do it if you tried hard enough!"

Ms. Achiever is confident in her teaching abilities and prefers to work independently of her colleagues. Given a choice, she would choose to teach in a totally self-contained classroom where little sharing of lessons and/or students is necessary because she is certain that if she does it herself, it will be done right. Her guiding premise is: If I succeed, I want the credit (status, prestige); if I fail, I will take full responsibility.

Acquiring a leadership position as an administrator is a professional goal for Ms. Achiever.

The Persuader

Mr. Persuader is a middle-school teacher who is responsible for teaching English and social studies classes. As you read about how she does things, ask yourself, "Does he have a counterpart at my school?"

Mr. Persuader is described by his students and peers as being one of the most enthusiastic and inspiring teachers in the school. It is said, "He has an unusual ability to get students excited and involved in any lesson he teaches, even the topics that normally are considered boring and irrelevant by this age group." His teaching style is entertaining and dramatic. He tends to act out everything he is communicating. Facial expressions, gestures, body language, and movement around the room are all part of the show. Humor, personal dreams, and anecdotes are used to maintain student attention.

Instructional lessons emphasize general concepts and their relationship to one's immediate environment. He is considered very eclectic and pragmatic. "Whatever works" is a central theme of his teaching. Attention to details and specific facts is a source of annoyance for him. This quality causes problems for those who work (and live) with him.

Mr. Persuader is astute about social environments and is intuitive about individual needs. He is careful not to move ahead on any plan unless a climate of readiness is evident. This is apparent both in and out of the classroom. What Mr. Persuader lacks in teaching strategies is compensated for by his enthusiastic and personal approach. Complaints from students indicate that he tends to belabor a point or over explain a concept long after it seems clear that everyone understands. He is too verbose at times.

Students gather around him wherever he goes. They enjoy sharing personal experiences and concerns with him and he takes time to listen. As a result, he usually is behind schedule on everything, especially reports that require detail. His fast-moving pace is what saves him.

Mr. Persuader never misses an opportunity to touch base with his colleagues in the teacher's lounge. He loves to discuss mutual interests and share his many successes with them. He values relationships. Attention and approval from peers are important to him. He makes an excellent fellow staff member because, in problem-solving situations, he fervently believes that solutions are always possible. Peers frequently appoint him to influential committees because he has their confidence in being able to win over most resisters. Sometimes, in his enthusiasm, he oversells what he realistically can deliver.

Mr. Persuader enjoys challenging assignments and rarely does the same thing twice in the same way. Freedom and change are valued highly by him. He detests and resists any administrative restraints on his academic freedom. He is good and he knows he is good! He likes to take risks by approaching tasks in colorful ways and it works for him.

Mr. Persuader's goal is to become a curriculum consultant or supervisor where he can travel from one school to another helping fellow teachers improve the quality of their instruction.

The Supporter

Miss Supporter is a third-grade teacher. As you read about how she does things, ask yourself, "Does he have a counterpart at my school?"

Miss Supporter's classroom atmosphere is relaxed and calm. She is attentive to individual needs and cares about how students are feeling about themselves and their work. She encourages students to express their thoughts and feelings freely; she reinforces their efforts by smiling, nodding approval, or using verbal encouragers like, "Good idea, Jon." Students always know where they stand with her because her facial expressions and body language readily communicate her approval and disapproval of their actions. Classroom walls display the students' assignments and drawings. Other displays include pictures of children, pets, flowers, and scenic views of beautiful sunsets.

Miss Supporter's teaching style involves asking open-ended questions with less emphasis on specific facts and details. While she encourages a broad range of views, she insists on mutual respect for other people's ideas so as to avoid conflict or hostile feelings within the group. On any issue, she does not hesitate to communicate her personal values and attitudes. Following extensive discussions where everyone has had an opportunity to participate, she moves toward achieving a consensus, all the while seeking ideal solutions to problems.

Miss Supporter is very patient with students. She provides a great deal of time for them to respond to questions. The pace of her lessons is slow. Students are expected to wait patiently, and they do. She will work endlessly with one student until they see the light. Miss Supporter makes physical contact with her students by sitting close to them, hugging them, or holding their hand. On the playground, her former students rush toward her to get their daily dose of approval.

Miss Supporter is perceived by her peers as being an excellent teacher, but she does experience considerable anxiety when any changes in school curriculum, organization, or policy are suggested. She believes that traditional approaches that have been used over time are best, so she strongly resists any efforts to implement change. As a result, she has an endless supply of activities because she never throws anything away.

In problem-solving situations she always asks, "What is best for our students?" She is often perceived as a crusader for the less fortunate and that concern is expressed by her diligent efforts to refer students for special services. She feels strongly that they will receive the special attention they need there.

Miss Supporter is valued highly as a staff member because of her willingness to get involved. Others say, "You can always count on her!" She has the unique ability to get along well with everyone no matter how disparate their individual views. She finds time to listen intently to everyone.

At times Miss Supporter expresses concern that no one seems to appreciate the efforts that teachers make. She feels that the principal is usually too busy to spend time visiting their rooms and parents are careless about helping their children with their homework assignments.

Ten years from now, Miss Supporter's goal is to be doing exactly what she is doing now because she loves children and knows she can provide comfortable environments for learning.

The Analyst

Mr. Analyst is a high school teacher who is responsible for teaching math and science. As you read about how he does things, ask yourself, "Does he have a counterpart at my school?"

Mr. Analyst presents information to students in a systematic, precise, and detailed manner. He is logical and organized when explaining concepts. It is obvious to everyone that he is well prepared and, consequently, he is considered to be an excellent teacher. He insists that students respond similarly by following procedures and directions exactly as explained.

Mr. Analyst sets high standards for himself and for his students. Heavy emphasis is placed on the scientific method. Inferences and conclusions must be based on observable and measurable data. He encourages independent research to find the right answers to important questions.

His classroom atmosphere is quiet and disciplined. Students work independently on assignments. When their work is completed accurately, they are expected to engage in quiet reading activities at their desks. Presentations by Mr. Analyst are described by students as being well organized but "somewhat dry" at times. There is not much student participation in class. Interpersonal contact with him during breaks is minimal. Bulletin boards contain diagrams and detailed illustrations of procedures for accomplishing complex tasks such as science experiments or mathematical calculations.

Mr. Analyst's approach to solving problems both in and out of school is cautious, logical, and persistent. When he puts his mind to something, he can be very single-focused and extremely precise. New or innovative approaches for accomplishing a task presented to him by students or peers are discouraged. He likes to go by the book. Even though he is considered to be hard-working, he never seems to get things done on time. There are long delays in student feedback regarding their projects or tests. If the principal assigns him the responsibility for investigating a problem, he seems to procrastinate endlessly until he is absolutely sure he has identified the right procedure to follow. During the process, he checks with his colleagues and the principal for reassurance that he is proceeding correctly.

Mr. Analyst does not interact much with his fellow teachers. No one really knows for sure how he feels about anything. They say he likes "to do his own thing." When the principal conducts a classroom observation, Mr. Analyst prefers feedback on the accuracy and logic of his content, not on his delivery. He views personal compliments with suspicion because he has been recognized in the past for his accomplishments, not as an individual.

Although parents and students consider him to be a very conscientious teacher, his goal is to enter a new career where he can spend more time investigating and conducting scientific research.

Now that you have spent considerable time and energy studying how you might identify interpersonal styles, the focus now will turn to strategies for working effectively with each style. Style-specific strategies are discussed in the next chapter.

THE MESSAGE

All styles can create greatness. People are all goal directed and needs driven. Effective consulting is predicated on the understanding, acceptance, and appreciation of the different styles. Collaborative work places can only occur when uniqueness and the strengths of each style are celebrated. It is a waste of your valuable time to wish that people were different or to hope they will change. Start learning how to identify styles so you can do what you believe is in everyone's best interest.

8

WORKING WITH STYLE

How do I work with them?
How do they work with me?

YOU CAN'T CROSS A BRIDGE UNTIL YOU COME TO IT. BUT AT LEAST TRY TO LAY DOWN A PONTOON OR TWO AHEAD OF TIME.

Everything we read related to improving the workplace tells us that people must work collaboratively if they are to make them challenging, exciting, fulfilling, and useful places to be. So the question is: How can people with different interpersonal styles work together to accomplish mutual goals, as well as meet their individual needs? The answer, in part, is:

♦ We all need to have a wide repertoire of strategies for interacting with all the different styles we will encounter.

♦ We need to be proactive, that is, we need to take the initiative, and anticipate the best way to work with people with different styles.

Being proactive does not mean being pushy or taking control. It means creating situations that are likely to lead to success for everyone. An error many people make, particularly if they are unfamiliar with a person or the situation, is to show up and hope for the best.

At no time should any strategy ever be used by anyone to manipulate people into doing what is not in their best interests. Strategies must be used sincerely for mutual benefits. If people sense that you are trying to maneuver them in some clandestine way, they will shut down. They should!

To be successful working with colleagues with different styles, it is helpful to remember that people do things for their reasons, to meet their needs, not yours. You are not center stage in their life. Prior to meeting with them, it may help to ask yourself these three questions:

1.   Whose need is it for us to meet, mine or theirs ?

2.   What is in it for them to spend their valuable time working with me?

3.   What are the consequences for me and for them if they choose not to meet or follow up on a plan?

If you can answer these questions in advance, you are bound for success. Hang on and enjoy the ride!

THE BASICS FOR ANY STYLE

Two basic ingredients critical to your success are often ignored when working with colleagues: (1) time and (2) place.

First, make sure that you have allocated sufficient time during any one meeting to nurture the relationship and achieve your objectives. If sufficient time is not allocated, people get frustrated. They believe that once again, their time has been wasted with no solutions in sight and we care more about the problem than the people involved.

The best outcomes, generally speaking, are rarely achieved quickly or under pressure. In too many instances, important decisions (often about people's lives) are made quickly just to get things done and get out. Avoid being victimized by timelines and deadlines, theirs and yours.

It is equally important to find a convenient time to meet. Time during the school day is usually best, unless otherwise requested, because it communicates the value and importance that is placed on communicating and consulting with colleagues. Also, when school time is used, it increases the probability that a plan in which much time has been invested will be implemented.

The second item—where would be the best place to meet—is equally important. Both people should select the best work environment for them. If it is a more formal problem-solving situation, avoid meeting in public places like the halls or in the lounge. An inappropriate setting can devalue a meeting's importance.

During the meeting, physically position yourself in a way that nonverbally communicates equal status. Avoid having a desk between you, and try not to have your chairs opposite one another. Try to envision (and position) yourself on the same side against a problem.

STYLE-SPECIFIC STRATEGIES

Without question, there are many interactive strategies that can be used successfully with most of the people most of the time. Fortunately, we are all more alike than we are different. The best strategies are Win/Win. When Win/Win strategies are used, everyone feels good about the decision and is committed to the plan of action. Covey (1989) says it best: "Win/Win is a belief in the Third Alternative. It is not your way or my way: it is a better way, a higher way (p. 207)." Win/Win is a mind-set and a heart-set that communicates the message that either everybody wins or nobody wins.

The best way to communicate a Win/Win attitude is to use strategies that are closely aligned with a person's style. Strategies must address emotional needs, as well as task needs. The best way to design Win/Win strategies is to:

- ◆ Know who you are and your particular style.
- ◆ Know who they are and their particular styles.
- ◆ Create and mix strategies that will satisfy everyone's needs.

It is probable that the strategies you customarily use to influence colleagues are the same strategies that you would like colleagues to use when they work with you. Either they are the only strategies we know, or we mistakenly believe that everybody is just like us. Unfortunately, this is not always the case. Despite our overwhelming similarities, there are differences. The differences that are the most difficult for us to cope with are when colleagues have our opposite style. For example, you are an Achiever and he is a Supporter, or you are a Persuader and she is an Analyst. These polar opposites do not share common frames of reference. When they meet, the challenge begins. It seems that each side secretly believes that their counterparts just landed here from outer space; they are definitely foreigners to the way we are used to doing things.

As you consider the strategies that are suggested for all the different styles, you will always feel most comfortable with the strategies that match your style. This makes sense. They fit you; they meet your needs. Similarly, you will be most comfortable working with people who share your style. Again, this makes sense. You have similar needs, values, motivations, and aspirations. You understand and can predict how they will behave and how they may feel.

If you want to be effective working with people who are different from you, it is essential that you listen first, then use strategies that are most appropriate for their style. In other words, adapt your strategies to the person you are with; do not try to adapt the person to your preferred way of doing things.

Style-specific strategies discussed in this section are primarily for the ideal types. As you know, most people are not that pure in their style of behaving. You will more frequently be dealing with mixed styles or a combination of styles, so it is always necessary to remain flexible.

It is now time to focus our attention on these style-specific Win/Win strategies, that is, strategies that are more unique to each of the interpersonal styles: the Achiever, the Persuader, the Supporter, and the Analyst.

STRATEGIES FOR WORKING WITH ACHIEVERS

Let us begin by refreshing our memory about Achievers. They are high risk-taking, low people-oriented individuals who are confident and decisive. They need to be in control of situations; they generally are forceful and direct when working with colleagues. The questions are:

◆ How do I work successfully with Achievers?
◆ How should others work with me, an Achiever?

Several strategies for successful interaction are:

1. Use the KISS principle (Keep It Short and Simple). As soon as you get their attention, act. Stick to the key issues. Avoid any personal needs that you may have to speculate, theorize, hypothesize, fantasize, or analyze. If you do these things, you will lose their attention. They are "bottom-line" people; they like to cut to the chase.

2. Be business-like and direct. Say what is on your mind. In other words, out with it! They respect people who tell it like it is. They neither want nor need a preamble. They believe it is a waste of their valuable time to talk about anything that is not directly related to the topic at hand. Avoid any personal needs that you may have to socialize before you get down to work.

3. Be punctual. If they set aside some of their valuable time for you, be there. Excuses, no matter how legitimate, do not sit well with them. They value efficient use of their time. They have been watching the clock as they are doing other things waiting for you to arrive.

4. Set timelines for your meeting. State how much time you believe it will take to get the job done, then check in with them. What do they think, and how much time have they allocated?

5. Begin the conversation by asking factual, here-and-now questions that imply clear goals and specific objectives.

6. Provide a clear picture of the results they can expect to achieve from any proposed action. This meets their needs for efficiency and accountability. Later, when they trust you, you can ask more open-ended questions.

7. When the goals and objectives are clear, discuss evaluation strategies and tools. You only have to discuss them, they do not want to design them. (Someone else will be expected to do that. It is not their cup of tea.) They need concrete evidence that the plan is working. Intuitive feelings about seeing change will not fly with them; they need hard evidence.

8. Actively listen to their ideas. They always have great ideas and plenty of them. Avoid telling them what to do. They like to be in control. You can, however, propose options for their consideration.

9. Paraphrase and clarify most of what they say. This communication strategy guarantees that you have accurately received their message. This will decrease any confusion about what they want. It will also increase their confidence in you. They will consider you competent if you are able to rephrase their thoughts. Often, they will indicate that they resent these Rogerian listening techniques, especially paraphrasing. Make it clear to them that any restatement you make is for their benefit. That is, it is their guarantee that you have heard what they need.

10. When it is appropriate, take a firm position on issues. They must sense that you are as strong as they are; otherwise, they will not feel comfortable relinquishing control, nor will they listen to you. In fact, they will run right over you if you let them. Do not be mistaken, their intent is not to hurt you; they are only trying to get their needs met, at your expense if necessary.

11. If queried, be an authority or be prepared to quote the experts who have studied the problem you are facing.

Clearly demonstrate that you have the capabilities and the resources to address the problem.

12. Propose logical and efficient action plans for their consideration, but remember to give them control over the final solution. Logical plans need to have face validity, that is, make sense to them on the surface. If you are discussing long-range plans, be sure to discuss how early results can be monitored. Efficiency means there will be little to no down time. All systems are go.

13. Prior to meeting with them, anticipate all the possible objections they might have to any possible plan you have in mind. Be prepared to answer their seemingly endless questions with specific facts and figures. They are more likely to trust you if they feel that you have done your homework.

14. Never fail to give them most or all of the credit for identifying and solving problems. Status is one of their primary needs.

15. Above all, be incisive. They respect colleagues who are sharp, forceful, effective, and can cut through the details to the heart of the matter. They respect people who are most like themselves. Always remember, they do not want or need the whole picture, they just want the big picture.

16. They love and use terms or phases like:

    ◆ Accountability
    ◆ Effectiveness
    ◆ Efficiency
    ◆ Ready, fire, aim
    ◆ Cut to the quick
    ◆ Get to the bottom line
    ◆ We will get the job done one way or another
    ◆ We need to shoot from the hip on this

Enjoy Achievers; you will learn a lot about problem solving and decision making by working with them. You do not always have to agree with them, but at least enjoy their confidence and masterful leadership skills.

STRATEGIES FOR WORKING WITH PERSUADERS

Let us begin by refreshing our memory about Persuaders. They are high risk-taking, people-oriented individuals who are high-spirited and social. They love to inspire and be inspired. They are generally articulate and intense. Their greatest needs are recognition and applause. So the questions are:

- ♦ How do I work successfully with Persuaders?
- ♦ How should others work with me, a Persuader?

Several strategies for successful interaction are:

1. Take the time to personalize yourself every time you meet with them. Do not be too serious or task oriented at first. Be open and visibly interested in them as people. They trust people who value people.

2. Acknowledge their importance, competence, humor, and friendliness. These qualities are of high value to them. They will bond with you immediately if you recognize their strengths. They must bond with you before they can work with you.

3. Explicitly invite them to share their feelings, opinions, and expertise. They have plenty of them. Actively listen by giving them plenty of positive verbal and nonverbal feed-back. They thrive on recognition and applause.

4. Appeal to their hopes, dreams, and fantasies of how things could be. They are very creative and visionary. They are the original dreamers of the world. Share your own feelings and enthusiasm about possibilities, when it is appropriate.

5. Try to elicit specific data from them for later problem solving. Facts and details are not their cup of tea so this will not be easy, but it is necessary. Be careful. Do not over-whelm and alienate them with your specific facts and de-

tails. Like their neighboring style, Achievers, Persuaders only need the big picture, not the whole picture. They pride themselves for being able to trust their intuition.

6. Present your ideas in an enthusiastic, optimistic, and persuasive manner. They love to sell and be sold. Offer incentives (special recognition) for comprehensive plans, if appropriate.

7. Encourage and present ideas that are innovative or adaptable. They love change. They pride themselves in being flexible and adaptive. Encourage and help them to take the time that is necessary to fully develop a viable plan. Otherwise, they will implement a partially-designed plan, and be discouraged later with the results do not meet their expectations.

8. Design evaluation strategies that are sensitive enough to show early benefits, for example, curriculum-based measures or portfolios with rubrics. If they do not see immediate change, they will impulsively jump to another idea.

9. If you need to quote experts, quote the ones who they are likely to know or are prominent in their field. They are fascinated by research, but are not likely to search out the facts themselves. Third party stories also are effective, particularly if they know the people and like them.

10. Put plans or agreements in writing immediately after they are summarized. This helps them to stay focused and on target—a difficult undertaking for most Persuaders.

11. Reaffirm your personal relationship frequently. You can do this by frequently following up on a plan to which you both agreed. Besides, they will need you to help them stay focused. It is so easy for them to get caught up in another new idea.

Enjoy Persuaders. You will learn a lot about the importance of being optimistic and enthusiastic by working with them. You do not always have to agree with them, but at least enjoy their free thinking and creative spirit.

STRATEGIES FOR WORKING WITH SUPPORTERS

Let us begin by refreshing our memory about Supporters. They are lower risk-taking, more people-oriented individuals who have high ideals and standards for everyone. They love calm environments; they hate conflict. Their greatest needs are to be appreciated and secure. So the questions are:

♦ How do I work successfully with Supporters?
♦ How should others work with me, a Supporter?

Several strategies for successful interaction are:

1. Never approach them in a cold, harsh, strictly business manner. Always break the ice with a personal comment. Try to stay calm, casual, friendly, and informal. That is how they are, at least on the surface.

2. Request their assistance. They love to help. It is their specialty. They enjoy finding problems and solving the problems with you.

3. Ask how questions: questions that elicit their opinion and allow you be aware of their values. Ask only open-ended questions at first because these questions are much less threatening to them. Closed questions often place more emphasis on facts and details.

4. Actively listen, then reflect their feelings and concerns. Be genuine with these responding skills because they will recognize insincerity immediately. They have a sixth sense about people. Provide positive verbal and nonverbal feedback. They must feel certain that you have heard their total story (facts and feeling) before they are willing to consider any options that you might propose.

5. Appreciate any efforts they have made thus far. They need to feel, first and foremost, that you have a sincere interest and concern for them as fellow human beings.

6. Discuss clear solutions to the problems they face and then discuss why these solutions might be appropriate. Be sure to demonstrate your awareness of the impact any decision can have on the total picture, particularly on the people it will affect.

7. Only discuss ideas that are consistent with their values and can meet their standards. They are the original idealists. Listen for their values, *really* listen for their values. For example, do not propose behavior-modification strategies unless you are sure that they fully understand the concepts. They may see external rewards as bribing people to do what is not in their best interests.

8. Use third party stories if you sense some apprehension about taking a risk. Trust will increase if you name fellow teachers that they respect and relate to. If you want to develop or maintain your credibility with Supporters, do not talk about all the successful Achievers you have known. Supporters are not like Achievers, nor do they want to be like them.

9. Listen patiently and attentively as they wrestle with making the right moral and ethical decisions. At some time in the future, it may be necessary to gently nudge them into a decision, but before doing so, make sure their fears have been acknowledged and that any risks will be shared.

10. Make it very easy for them to share their objections and to say exactly what is on their minds, otherwise, they will not do it. They hate conflict and disappointing people. They want everybody to be happy and get along. They can easily fool you into believing that they are with you, intellectually and emotionally, when they are not. They have the unique ability to outwardly accept, yet inwardly reject, ideas. They will smile and nod, but covertly disagree and you will never know it! The benefits for you to encourage them to speak openly without consequences about their fears and concerns, is that you can only deal with their issues if you know

what they are. And, by the way, their fears and concerns are very legitimate. They are intuitive about people problems.

11. Get a written commitment to any intervention plans. Because they hate change and conflict, and therefore will avoid it like the plague, get something in writing. Assure them that any plan can be negotiated and altered to meet their standards and values. When they feel comfortable with a plan, they will see it through to completion because they are very dependable.

12. Frequently touch base with them. They need to feel your commitment and to have your personal assurances that things will work out to everyone's benefit.

Enjoy Supporters. You will learn a lot about being a good listener and putting people first by working with them. You do not always have to agree with them, but at least enjoy their idealism and integrity.

STRATEGIES FOR WORKING WITH ANALYSTS

Let us begin by refreshing our memory about Analysts. They are lower risk-taking, low people-oriented individuals who are highly disciplined and persistent. They love to reason and to have time to think things through. Their greatest needs are for accuracy and order. So the questions are:

♦ How do I work successfully with Analysts?
♦ How should others work with me, an Analyst?

Several strategies for successful interaction are:

1. Be reserved, but not cold, when you approach them. They are awkward with light, social conversations until they get to know you. If you must stay light, be prepared to carry the conversation.

2. Arrive on time. They truly believe that clocks were created for a reason. You will lose credibility if you cannot be

punctual. Be prepared to get down to business immediately. They are very task oriented.

3. Present information in a logical, step-by-step manner and take plenty of time doing it. That is how they think, so match it.

4. Pay close attention to details. If you do not, they will. (They are sometimes described as nit-picky.) Take detailed notes of what people say because details are important to them. Each and every detail will need to be addressed in the final plan if you want their support.

5. Appeal to logic, reason, order, and a scientific approach to solving a problem. In other words, be systematic, precise, thorough, structured, and disciplined. You can never be too logical for them. They are more likely to trust people who use the phrases such as:

   ◆ "Logic would dictate . . . ."
   ◆ "Reason would suggest . . . ."
   ◆ "The data clearly indicates . . . ."
   ◆ "Research findings are clear . . . ."

6. Be completely prepared. Research or study the problem or issue in advance. Collect reams of data on it. They may not tell you this outright, but in their heart of hearts, they truly believe that the person with the most data wins. In other words, do your homework if you want them to trust you.

7. Be prepared to discuss and suggest several viable alternatives. Then get ready to evaluate each and every one of them. It is important for them to find the right one, not just the best one.

8. Expect to be challenged on your assumptions, intuitions, ideas, and procedures. Do not personalize these challenges; They have nothing to do with you. They love to analyze and criticize ideas. In fact, they are the original "Yes, but . . . ." people. The good news is that you can count on them to

discover things that you may have overlooked or any errors you may have made.

9.   Present ideas and strategies that are consistent with known policies and procedures. They like to stick by the book. That way, their work is unlikely to come under any criticism by their superiors.

10.   Set specific, clear timelines for each step of an intervention plan; otherwise, they get bogged down in details and have a hard time setting themselves free. Timelines meet their need for order and predictability. Ironically, they will spend hours creating time-management charts.

11.   Analyze the long-range effects of any proposed ideas. Give them time to mull things over. They need to be thorough. Time to verify the reliability and validity of any decisions is essential to their mental health.

12.   Use objective and sensitive measurement procedures for gauging the efficacy of any plan. They need to be sure they are getting accurate, concrete, precise, and practical results from their efforts. Ongoing data analyses is important to them. Graph the results so they can see the benefits. Graphs, maps, charts, or anything with numbers thrill them, so try to use them.

13.   Be persistent. Every decision will take a long time. Keep your composure as you proceed.

14.   Expect to receive very little feedback, either verbally or nonverbally, unless you specifically ask (and wait) for a response. Volunteering anything is not their forte, but you can be sure that they have an opinion, as well as the data to support it.

15.   Minimize risks for them. Anticipate all the worst case scenarios and how they can be solved. Risks and surprises frighten them, so decrease the probability of any occurring.

Enjoy Analysts. You will learn a lot about long-range planning and quality control by working with them. You do not always have to agree with them, but appreciate their industriousness and attention to detail.

THE MESSAGE

Because considering an array of strategies is a necessary and integral part of consulting and communicating, take the time to think about your collaborators and what they might want from you. Equally important, take time to understand your own needs. When you figure out how to mix and mesh your styles, you will have designed strategies that can work for both of you. By considering the most appropriate strategies with each type of person—the Achiever, the Persuader, the Supporter, or the Analyst—you are more likely to get the job done as well as have people feel good about the process. What else can we ask for?

LIFE IS A DARING ADVENTURE OR NOTHING AT ALL!

SUCCESSFUL CONSULTING

What makes it successful?
What do I need to do more of?

think of a time when you consulted with a colleague and the experience left you with a warm glow. Was it because you left the situation with the information you needed, or was it because of the positive feelings you had about yourself and the person with whom you were working? Before you read this chapter, take a few minutes to reflect on what you think made the whole experience so worthwhile. What happened during your time together that made it so successful for you?

Reflect on what you have read in the previous chapters. What factors did you connect with? What made sense to you? As you read this chapter, compare your notes with what is written in the pages ahead. This chapter will review many of the critical factors that make consulting efforts successful, as well as remind us of what we need to pay more attention to if we are not experiencing the joy that we so rightfully deserve as we work with colleagues.

As you thought about what made your consulting experiences successful, you may have been tempted to think, "Consulting is most successful when I work with people who are most like me." We all know those people; they think and act just like us. For example, they believe that whole-language instruction (or direct instruction) is the only way to teach, and so do you. They believe that active involvement (or limited involvement) of students in instructional and behavioral management decisions is the only way to do it, and so do you. You both believe that these practices are the best way, the right way. Granted, it may be easier to work with your soul mates, but it may not necessarily be more successful. In fact, it may be that you are both wrong in your thinking about a particular situation and are reinforcing each other's erroneous beliefs. It helps occasionally to get fresh ideas by working and learning from people who are different than you in several dimensions like interpersonal style, comfort level with risk-taking, organizational skills, intuition, holistic/global approaches, interactive approaches, or instructional styles.

There are a number of factors that influence the success of consulting. Let us review some of the factors that have been examined in previous chapters:

1. You use a problem-solving process to guide your discussion.

2. You pay as much attention to the process (the how) as the product (the what).

3. Communication skills are the glue that holds the process together.

4. We expend our efforts during problem solving and planning on things we can change: our circle of influence, not our circle of concern (Covey, 1989).

Additional factors, about which there is general agreement, are discussed in the pages ahead. Many of these factors were learned, often the hard way, through the author's own experiences consulting with individuals and organizations for over 20 years. The hours spent observing and training people in the consulting process are invaluable to growth. Much of what the author has learned came as a direct result of being in the role of a consultee, both as a classroom teacher and as someone who is constantly seeking advice from colleagues.

RAPPORT AND TRUST ARE ESTABLISHED

The importance of trust when working with colleagues cannot be overstated. Trust makes the world go around. Trust is what allows us to enter other people's worlds. The best recommendations or agreements are doomed to failure if trust is absent. When trust is high, cooperation is more stable and communication is more effective. People express their emotions, opinions, and ideas more openly when the trust level is high. When the trust level is low, people are evasive, dishonest, and inconsiderate in their dealings with others. Trust is at the heart of consulting efforts.

Establishing trust is very complex. It does not just happen suddenly; you have to work hard to earn it. During the initial stages of consulting when trust is typically low, try to develop rapport and connections with people. You can develop connections in two ways: (1) Attend to their interpersonal styles by addressing their emotional needs, and (2) Synchronize with them by trying to match their body positions (posture and gestures), facial expressions, breathing, voice (tone, tempo, pitch, volume, and intonation), and word patterns (Bandler & Grinder, 1975). When you begin with these, other things start to fall in place.

Before we discuss basic strategies for gaining trust, let us first look at how you evaluate the trustworthiness of your friends and colleagues. You probably ask yourself questions similar to these:

◆ Do I truly believe in my solar plexus that they have my best interests at heart as well as their own, or do I sense a hidden agenda even though I cannot identify it yet?

◆ Do their actions match their words, or is there incongruity between what they say and what they do? For example, do they say that they value my opinion and then not really listen to me?

◆ Can I trust them with the truth about how I really feel, or will what I say be used against me now or in the future?

♦ Am I hearing a Win/Win approach to solving this problem, or am I hearing how the problem can be solved at my expense?

These are the same questions that others are asking of you as you interact with them. Whenever you feel that you do not have trust with people, ask these same questions from their perspective.

Trust is largely a feeling. When you have trust, you feel it. When you do not have trust, you sense it. So how do you develop trust when you do not feel that you have it? In a nutshell, you gain trust with people when you manifest these behaviors:

♦ Empathy
♦ Acceptance
♦ Credibility

Empathy is the ability to understand how someone else is feeling. It is developed by mentally and emotionally projecting yourself into the other person's world and asking yourself questions such as:

♦ How might he or she be feeling right now?
♦ How would I be feeling if I was in his or her place?
♦ What questions would I be asking myself?
♦ What concerns would I have?
♦ How would I want to be treated in this situation?

Acceptance is expressed by showing a positive high regard for people's strengths, uniqueness, contributions, and ability to productively manage situations. You respect their points-of-view and accept their feelings as rational and justifiable. You view and accept things as they really are, not as you may wish them to be. No attempt is made to impose your beliefs, values, or opinions on others. Genuine respect for them as fellow human beings is communicated. Relationships are open and equal.

Acceptance does not mean that you agree or are giving them your unconditional approval. It only communicates an acceptance of their attitudes (beliefs, feelings, and behavior) from their frame of reference. It essentially means that you get inside their bodies, their minds, and hearts and see things through their eyes and relate to their experiences.

Credibility has essentially three components: propriety, competence, and communicating intent. People evaluate your propriety when they ask themselves questions such as:

- ◆ Is he what he says he is?
- ◆ Is she like me?
- ◆ Can I relate to him?
- ◆ Are we compatible?
- ◆ Is she my kind of person?

The more similar you are, the higher the trust level. In addition, the more competence you demonstrate, the higher the trust level. People evaluate your competence when they ask themselves questions such as:

- ◆ Does he have the expertise to get the job done?
- ◆ Is she experienced?
- ◆ Does he have the qualifications?
- ◆ Can she understand our situation?

The third way to establish credibility is to openly communicate your intent and motives. This often is accomplished through self-disclosure. You say, in essence, "Here is who I am. Here is what I am feeling. Here is what I am thinking." People evaluate your intent when they ask themselves questions such as:

- ◆ Is he open, sensible, and sharing?
- ◆ Is she likely to be flexible?
- ◆ Is he likely to care about us?
- ◆ Does she have a Win/Win attitude?

You build trust by creating expectations for others and you create expectations by communicating your intent. When consulting, you state what you hope to achieve during your time together, how you perceive your role, how you perceive their role, the planning and problem-solving process that you would like to use, and your concern for their involvement in every decision that is made.

During the early stages, when you are building trust, try to communicate confidence by feeling confident. Confidence comes from believing that there are any number of ways to solve a problem, and that you are not solely responsible for finding a solution. Believe that whatever the problem is, it can be solved if it is approached collaboratively.

Trust is a great tranquilizer. It allows people to stay calm and focused. Through all the phases of consulting, continuously ask yourself these two questions: "Am I paying enough attention to people and not just the problem?" and "Are my actions earning their trust?"

Once trust is established, all things are possible—not guaranteed, just possible!

ACCEPT PEOPLE AS THEY ARE

So easy to say, so difficult to do. If we are committed to working with colleagues, we need to accept them as they are and stop wishing they were different. People are what they are, and they are not likely to change to any significant degree (at least not in our time with them). It may save valuable energy to remember these little three pieces of wisdom:

1. People are dancing as fast as they can. Their ability to perform is based on their resources at this point in their lives. Resources are both internal and external. They include experiences, physical energy, time, creativity, self-esteem, and support from significant others.

2. All people strive toward excellence as they see it and on their schedule, not on ours.

3. People who are different from us can push our thinking. They can help us become the best of what we want to be if we remain open to the experience.

If we can accept people as they are and learn from them, trust will flourish and stress will decrease. What a gift!

THINK WITH, NOT FOR, AND NOT AT COLLEAGUES

One of the definitions of consulting in any standard dictionary is to deliberate together, or to confer with others. This means that you think with people when consulting. You bounce ideas off each other to create deeper understandings and new insights. The results are higher quality solutions to implement.

One of the most difficult aspects of consulting is to resist thinking for people and to resist giving them your solutions. When you think for them, consultees can feel that you are sticking your answers on them like self-stick notes (and before too long, they generally all fall off). Out of genuine kindness and concern, we want to help people and save them from the pain of learning; learning the old-fashioned way: through experience. Is it possible that discovery learning, in a structured environment, may be the best way, the more exciting way, and the most enduring way for all of us, teachers and students alike?

The consequences of thinking for people are obvious. We keep people dependent on us. While it is initially reinforcing to our egos to have answers for other people, eventually, we lose more than we gain. Dependency has an erosive quality; people feel demeaned by it, and over time, lose self-esteem because they cannot count on their own abilities. They come to believe that other people are smarter and better at solving problems than they are. Sooner or later, they come to wonder why these smart people just do not take care of these tough problems on their own in the first place. Dependency jeopardizes opportunities for learning and empowerment. Furthermore, when people are dependent on us, they require more of our limited time. We often come to resent this dependency later.

You can catch yourself thinking for people when you hear yourself saying things such as:

- ♦ "Here is what you need to do!"
- ♦ "If I were you, I would . . . ."
- ♦ "What you should do is . . . ."
- ♦ "Why not just do this . . . ?"

The worst practice is to think *at* people. When you do this, you give the appearance of running right over them. You jump in early before the problem or issue is clear and bombard them with a barrage of options which leaves them confused and, at times, angry.

The consequences of thinking at people is that you put people on the defensive. Your first clue that you are doing this is when you hear people saying more often than you would like, "Yes, but . . . ," or "I agree with you, however . . . ." These phrases may be their way of saying, "Until I believe that you understand my situation, I will be stone deaf to your ideas, no matter how great they are!"

THE MANTRA: THE PROCESS YIELDS THE PRODUCT

Consulting occurs at two levels: content and process. On one level, you address the content of the problem; on the other, you focus, usually implicitly, on the process for delivering the content. For example, the content level of consulting may involve a teacher's request for assistance in managing a student's problem behavior in the classroom. Here, curriculum knowledge, experience, and behavioral-management strategies are required.

The second and more critical level—process—involves how you will work with the person to find a solution to his or her request. At this level, knowledge regarding interpersonal styles and communication skills are essential. Without these skills, you may never get a chance to share your content expertise because no one is listening. If you wish to consult effectively with colleagues, you must remember one recurring theme: The process yields the product.

People who are viewed by their peers as being highly successful when consulting with colleagues are able to magically integrate both process and content during problem solving. It is possible for the process to escape notice by the untrained eye because it usually occurs at an automatic and often unconscious level.

ATTEND TO PEOPLE'S READINESS TO LEARN

When consulting with colleagues, be very sensitive to when people are truly requesting technical assistance and when they only want to vent their feelings. In the latter situation, actively listen until a readiness to act is clearly indicated. If you are unsure, ask questions such as:

◆ "Is there anything you would like to do to change things?"
◆ "Is there any way I can help?"

These questions generally clarify what people really want. If they are not ready for technical assistance at this time, their response is usually something like, "No, I just needed to talk to someone."

Readiness to learn is related to a need-to-know, a knowledge base for assimilating the new information, and an experiential base for understanding the information. Four learning levels need to be considered when problem solving with colleagues. The first level is a prerequisite to the second and so on. They are:

◆ Awareness
◆ Knowledge
◆ Application
◆ Generalization

People need to be aware that a condition or a strategy exists before they are ready to acquire knowledge about it. Knowledge of a skill or strategy precedes the ability to apply it. And, finally, with a conscious effort and repeated applications in a variety of situations, generalization occurs. You may need to provide support through this entire sequence before you can discontinue your involvement. Initially, however, you must determine at which level people are currently functioning on the issue that is being addressed and begin there. These levels, used in sequence, make it possible to set realistic expectations and timelines for change, thereby avoiding disappointment and frustration for all concerned.

A useful strategy in situations like this is to listen actively to what they know now, then piggy-back on one of their ideas by discussing in more detail an intervention that they already know or have tried.

In this way, you have some assurance that they have a level of readiness for understanding the options that are proposed.

ACCEPT WHO ULTIMATELY HAS CONTROL

Both parties, the consultant and the consultee, develop, clarify, and evaluate ideas together, but in the final analysis, after all the data have been gathered and analyzed, the consultee has the final responsibility for accepting, rejecting, or modifying any recommendations. When in the role of a consulting teacher, never try to exercise control over colleagues or demand mentally that they conform to your expectations. When the situation demands that you must mutually agree, new alternatives should be pursued, even when you believe that the recommendations discussed would work. The final decision is always the consultee's because he or she is ultimately responsible for implementing the program; therefore, it must be a personal fit.

CLARIFY EXPECTATIONS EARLY

It is not unusual for people to believe that individuals who serve as consultants are experts with quick and easy answers. This expectation not only puts a great deal of pressure on you if you are in that role, but it also creates false expectations in them about what may happen. Therefore, expectations must be identified and discussed early in the process. Expertise myths need to be dispelled. It is important to clarify what your role is and what it is not.

Sometimes these expectations are directly related to a consultee's need for immediate relief; that is, he or she wants you to have simple, easy recipes to follow. Even though there is a strong temptation to respond immediately to his or her plea for help and do something now, it is best not to get trapped into providing an immediate solution. To temporarily satisfy an urgent need, engage in active listening, gather assessment data, or employ a diagnosis-by-intervention strategy. In the third option, you help consultees see that this approach is just as it says: an intervention strategy is implemented to confirm or reject diagnostic hypothesis. The medical profession uses this strategy all the time. They prescribe a drug (solution) and closely monitor its effects. The intervention may be only temporary. The program is altered and adapted as new data is collected and analyzed.

Consultees need to learn, as we all do, that there are rarely any easy, quick and easy solutions. Each situation, each student, and each consultee is unique. Considerable time must be spent on problem finding if the best solution is to be found.

COMMUNICATE IN DIFFERENT PERCEPTUAL MODES

Much misunderstanding occurs as a result of people assuming that colleagues learn and think in the same way that they do. In actuality, we all process information and attempt to make sense of things through our dominant perceptual mode or representational system (Grinder & Bandler, 1976). The three modes or systems by which we organize our experiences are:

◆ The visual system
◆ The auditory system
◆ The haptic/tactile system

Each of us has a dominant mode to which other modes are secondary. If you are a visual thinker and communicator, you create mental images for yourself and prefer that others create word pictures when communicating with you. If you are an auditory thinker and communicator, you prefer to think in phrases and words, either overtly (by thinking aloud) or covertly (by an inner voice). In contrast to visual and auditory people is the haptic thinker and communicator. This individual appears to have a heightened sense of physical awareness: a sense of emotion, an intuition, or felt inferences, that seem to transcend the normal cognitive processes. It is reported that when Louis Armstrong was asked to explain jazz, he replied, "If you cannot feel it, you cannot understand it." The sculptor, Rodin, probably felt the same way.

When we communicate with colleagues, it is important that we use their dominant perceptual mode, especially during the initial stages when rapport and trust is likely to be low. Even though this requires more effort and planning on your part, the results are well worth it for these reasons: (1) you will reach more people, (2) people will have a clearer understanding of what you are trying to communicate, and (3) it will save time in the long run. Later on, the dominant mode can be supplemented using the secondary ones.

Consider this exchange between Michael and Marilee. As you read it, pay attention to the signal words that alert you to their dominant perceptual mode:

> Michael: "Marilee, I really do not *see* how this particular strategy can help these students. Can you *show* me why I should use it?"
>
> Marilee: "Michael, I do not know how I can *say* much more than I have already. What is it exactly that you would like to have me *reexplain*?"
>
> Michael: "I do not know for sure. It is just that the strategy does not *look* feasible to me."
>
> Marilee: "Try using it, Michael. I can just *hear* the enthusiasm in your students already."
>
> Michael: "Well, I guess I will have to spend more time trying to get a *picture* of this for myself. I will call you when I get it figured out."

As you can see, Michael and Marilee have a disconnection between their perceptual modes. One could argue that their computers are not compatible. Each received an error message that said, in essence, "Disk does not read." Both Michael and Marilee revealed important information about their dominant modes for assimilating information. Michael wants to *see* how Marilee's strategies would benefit him, while Marilee is trying to help Michael *hear* his student's enthusiasm. They are speaking different languages, and neither one appears to be aware of the source of the communication problem. The simplest way to identify a person's dominant mode is to listen for the cue words and then use that person's mode as much as possible when communicating. The following phases further illuminate the three different modes by suggesting key words that people might use when conversing with colleagues:

Visual Mode

+ "I *see* what you mean."
+ "That idea *looks* good to me."
+ "Show me the big *picture*."
+ "My point of *view* is. . . ."
+ "Can you put that in *writing*?"

Auditory Mode

+ "*Tell* me again."
+ "Did I *hear* you say. . . ?"
+ "That idea *sounds* fishy to me."
+ "I need a *sounding* board for this idea."
+ "*Explain* that again."

Physical/Tactile Mode

+ "That concept *feels* right."
+ "I am *feeling* uneasy about . . . ."
+ "My *sense* is that . . . ."
+ "The idea does not *sit* right with me."
+ "My *gut feelings* suggest . . . ."

When you are communicating information to colleagues, it helps to pause periodically and ask them questions using their dominant mode. Here are some examples:

+ "Does this plan *look/sound/feel* okay to you?"
+ "Can you *see* yourself doing this?"
+ "How does this idea *sound/feel/appear* to you?"
+ "Does this *answer* the questions you have been *asking*?"
+ "How do you *feel* about the plan so far?"
+ "How does this information *fit* for you?"
+ "What is your *sense* of this?" (This one is open for all modes to respond.)

The message is clear. You can heighten people's receptivity to an idea by presenting it in a way that they can either see, hear, and/or feel the benefits of your ideas. By so doing, effective communication can be increased dramatically.

OPPORTUNITIES ARE PROVIDED FOR REFLECTION IN, ON, AND ABOUT PRACTICE.

Can you remember times when you have sought out the help of a colleague, not because you wanted answers (at least, not yet), but because you wanted some time to think out loud, to question, to self-question, and to reflect on and about what you are doing and why you are doing it? As the rate of information explodes and the curriculum expands, increasingly we feel a need to ask ourselves questions like, "What is really important to teach and what do I need to let go? I cannot teach it all even though I think I should!"

Teaching is rife with pressure. It moves at a rapid pace and there are so many things to be done. There are always new units to develop, new lessons to plan, decisions to make, meetings to attend, students' needs to meet, and parents to call. Consulting with colleagues can help relieve this constant pressure. It allows time to get back in touch with your deepest needs, values, and feelings. It provides opportunities to articulate your inner voice and purposes, as well as review and evaluate what you are doing now that relates to students' needs. Most of all, it provides an opportunity to check your sanity by getting another perspective from people who do what you do daily and seem to have a grasp on how to survive with meaning and dignity.

IT OCCURS OVER A PERIOD OF TIME

Consulting is rarely a one-shot process, although it occasionally may be. More often, it occurs over a period of time because problems are rarely as simple as they initially appear. The process begins when there is a difference between what a person wants to have happening and what currently exists. Typically, the consultee determines when the process begins and when it will terminate. The process terminates either when the problem is solved or when the consultee feels confident enough to continue the program without further assistance. During this interval, there are frequent contacts between the consultee and the consultant. The actual number of contacts are mutually determined, but frequent follow ups after the initial meeting are critical if joint responsibility for change is the mutual agreement.

THERE IS DISTRICT-LEVEL SUPPORT

Unless district-level and building-level administrators value and visibly promote consultation among teachers, the process will not be used by teachers over time and to the degree that substantive changes are obvious. There must be top-down administrative support for bottom-up implementation efforts.

Administrators have the power (direct and indirect) and responsibility to involve all key stakeholders in designing how teachers will co-consult. They can help achieve consensus around the following issues: determining the need for consulting, designing a process for consulting, and identifying strategies for evaluating the effectiveness of consulting as a professional development activity. Administrators also have the power to arrange for time during the school day for teachers to consult with one another around school-related or student-related issues.

In some schools, there may not be administrative support during the initial stages of implementing a consulting model, but this is not a good reason for not starting. Sometimes you just have to get into the practice any way you can and, as you do it, collect data and feedback on its efficacy. Later, provide the findings to administrators and other stakeholders and engage them in a discussion. If the data are positive and come from respected colleagues, people are more likely to buy into the practice. Bottom line, everybody wants to be a winner, or be associated with people who behave like winners.

DeBoer & Fister (in press) suggest several ways for teachers to gain the support of their administrators. Five of the eighteen are listed below:

1. Do not hesitate to say, "I need your support," then be prepared to explain what support looks like to you. Be clear and specific in terms of what needs to happen for administrators to demonstrate support. For example, if you need

them to publicly articulate support for that innovation or practice, say so.

2. When presenting an idea, have or offer to create a tentative plan. Be sure your personal vision accompanies the idea or request. Try to submit plans that have goals, objectives, a rationale, benefits to all the stakeholders, and implementation strategies because they have the highest potential for success.

3. Select easy-to-read articles, preferably from administrators' journals, that describe the idea you want to convey. Make an appointment to discuss the information after they have read it.

4. When additional resources are needed, have ideas and solutions on how they can be secured. For example, how might time, money, or existing personnel be reconceptualized?

5. Communicate the importance of collaborative work cultures such as peer coaching, collegial problem solving, collaborative planning, and cooperative learning structures when implementing change. Be prepared to expend the effort to get things rolling.

CHANGES OCCUR AT MACRO AND MICRO LEVELS

Consulting in schools can be implemented at three different, but interrelated, levels:

- ◆ Level I: Indirect service to the student.
- ◆ Level II: Direct service to the teacher.
- ◆ Level III: Indirect service to the school system.

There are subtle but distinct differences between the three levels of consulting. Indirect service to the student (Level I) seeks to change student behavior as a result of interventions carried out by the problem initiator. Direct service to the teacher (Level II) aims to change the behavior of teachers by focusing on such things as instructional strategies, behavioral-analysis skills, or motivational techniques.

Indirect service to a school system (Level III) aims at identifying and intervening in situations where either the curriculum or the organization of the school is causing the problem. Both of these factors can create or perpetuate a system's problem. This category of consulting usually results in the most far reaching changes and should be considered as the ultimate goal of consulting in most situations.

The following example of consulting with a school district illustrates how these categories can work in actual practice in an integrated fashion. A superintendent requested the assistance of a consultant because a number of elementary teachers were concerned about the high incidence of students who were experiencing reading problems in their general education classrooms. It was the teachers' belief that instructional aides were necessary if these students were to be brought up to grade level. The teachers felt they did not have sufficient time to spend on individualizing instruction, which, to them, meant one-on-one instruction for each student. The superintendent was equally concerned with the problem but was more concerned about finding a more cost-effective solution that would yield long-range benefits for students, teachers, and the entire school district.

Entry to the system was made at Level I (indirect service to the student) by assisting the teachers in collecting the informal assessment data about student performance that was required for problem solving. At the same time, individual and small group problem-solving meetings, and mini-inservices were conducted with teachers over lunch hour and after school to develop and implement strategies such as whole-language instruction, literature-based instruction, and peer-mediated instruction (a Level II intervention).

The end result was that a Level III change was made to solve the problem. Several interventions were implemented. Because a reading series that was almost exclusively phonetically based had been adopted by the district, all those students whose primary learning style was not in concert with the textbooks' and the teachers' instructional strategies, were experiencing failure. The teachers decided to continue using the current reading series, but adapt their instruction to include a whole language or linguistic approach for some students. Thus, teaching strategies were more closely matched with learning styles.

Additional changes in Level II involved designing management systems with teachers that they, in turn, taught students. As a result, students learned how to use self-monitoring strategies for evaluating their own learning styles, on-task behaviors, and reading progress.

Approaching problems on these three different levels reverses the traditional framework for looking at problems. Instead of assuming that it is an inside-the-head problem and doing assessment and intervention with the student only, this approach assumes that a problem is caused by a combination of factors which include out-side-the-head factors such as the classroom environment, instructional strategies, district curriculum, and school organizational patterns and choices.

When consulting, you can approach a problem at any level. Consulting works best, at any level, when it is teacher-initiated. Teachers have the power to make changes in student behavior, their own behavior, and the way the school operates. Consulting that impacts the school system (Level III) should always be the focus because it has the highest potential for effecting long-range benefits for all students.

USE YOUR PERSONAL POWER IN APPROPRIATE AND ACCEPTABLE WAYS

Many people mistakenly believe that power is evil and claim to have no needs to accumulate it. But everyone needs power; power is the capacity to get things done and to make things happen. It enables people to alter their conditions so they can achieve their goals and meet their emotional needs. As such, power is neither good nor bad, moral or immoral, ethical or unethical. It is a neutral force like the wind or electricity. It can be used in ethical ways to acquire a better life, or it can be used unethically as a destructive force to hurt others.

Powerless people are apathetic and frustrated because they believe they cannot make a difference. They make statements like, "You cannot get people to change," or "They will not let me." Eventually, powerless people become hostile because they constantly feel victimized by other people's control over them. Anyone who claims to love himself or herself wants and needs power. The question is: How do you get it?

Much of our personal power is based on perception. We are all familiar with this common statement: "If you believe you have got it, then you have got it. If you believe you do not have it, you are probably right." A sense of well being and self-confidence communicates an image of power. Additional strategies for acquiring power available to everyone include:

◆ A willingness to take risks.
◆ Having expertise in an area in which people need information.
◆ Analyzing people's real needs vs. their stated needs.
◆ Actively listening to what people are saying.
◆ Developing rapport and trust with people.
◆ Getting people involved in a plan.
◆ Communicating legitimacy (e.g., the law, a mandate, or district policy).
◆ Arranging incentives (i.e., what is in it for them).
◆ Structuring both positive and logical consequences.
◆ Being associated with people who have power.
◆ Being persistent.

Persistence is a powerful strategy that is often ignored. It can be enhanced by using a technique called spaced repetition. If you want to influence someone's beliefs or behavior, it is important that you tell them repeatedly in subtle ways until they hear. When they finally do hear, they will often believe it is their own original idea. (When this happens, curb your tendency to say, "That is what I have been trying to tell you!") When it is appropriate, say, "What a great idea. I wish I had thought of that myself!"

When you are faced with a very difficult situation, you can deceive yourself into believing that you are totally powerless and cannot effect any change. But this is fallacious because you always have power. Cohen (1980) illustrates this concept very well in this story:

Imagine a prisoner in solitary confinement. The authorities have removed his shoe laces and his belt, because they don't want him to hurt himself . . . . The wretch slouches back and forth in his cell, holding up his pants with his left hand, not only because he's minus a belt, but because he's minus fifteen pounds. The food they shove under the steel door is slop, and he refuses to eat it. But now, as he runs his fingertips over his ribs, his nostrils pick up the scent of a Marlboro cigarette, his favorite brand.

Through a tiny porthole in the door, he watches as the lone guard in the corridor sucks in a lungful, then exhales blissfully. Desperate for a cigarette, the prisoner respectfully taps on the door with the knuckles of his right hand.

The guard ambles over and contemptuously grunts, "Whaddya want?"
The prisoner replies, "I'd like a cigarette, please . . . the kind you're smoking: a Marlboro."
The guard mistakenly perceives the prisoner as powerless, so he snorts derisively and turns his back.

The prisoner perceives his situation differently. He's aware of his options; he's willing to test his assumptions and take risks. So he taps again on the door with the knuckles of his right hand, this time commandingly.
The guard, exhaling a cloud of smoke, irritatedly turns his head. "Now whatddya want?"
The prisoner responds, "Please, I would like one of your cigarettes within the next thirty seconds. If I don't get it, I'm going to bang my head against the concrete wall till I'm a bloody mess and unconscious. When the prison officials pick me off the floor and revive me, I'll swear you did it. Now, they'll never believe me, but think of all the hearings you'll have to attend and the commissions you'll be testifying before. Think of the administrivia you'll be tangled in—**all that as opposed to giving me one crummy Marlboro!** Just one cigarette, and I promise not to bother you again."   Does the guard slip him a cigarette through the tiny peephole? Yes. Does he light it for him?

> Yes. Why? Because the guard has done a fast cost-benefit
> analysis of the situation (p. 53-54). ◌

Your circumstances, no matter how difficult, are probably much better than the prisoner's. You can change things if you believe you have power, take risks, spend time problem finding and problem solving, pay attention to people's emotional needs, remain patient, and have a repertoire of strategies for helping people change that you can use flexibly and adaptively.

HAVE PASSION FOR WHAT YOU ARE DOING

While all of the previous factors contribute to your success, one of the most important factors is having a passion for what you are doing and being excited about the learning opportunities ahead of you. Skills can influence your competence, but passion influences your destiny. Passion ignites everyone around you and provides a primary source of "fuel," especially during the tough times.

Passionate people are enthusiastic, inspiring, and dynamic. They have fire in their hearts. They believe passionately in what they are doing. Their work is a large part of their raison-d'être. Their commitment to what they are doing enables them to tap into their inner strengths, existing resources, personal abilities, and reserve energies.

Passionate people do not have to convince themselves to persevere, to stick with it. They have to convince themselves not to! Their work is not something they have to do; it is something they want to do.

Kriegel & Patler (1991) argue that anyone who rates what they are doing lower than a seven on a passion index of one to ten should either take time to get more fired up or change what they are doing. It is our positive energy that encourages people to communicate, collaborate, and consult with us.

THE MESSAGE

Consulting and collaborating with colleagues is an adventure—an adventure in learning. We learn many things: we learn about ourselves; we learn about how to create successful relationships; we learn about a process for solving problems; and we learn new strategies for creating success for students.

There are a number of things that we can do to create an environment for successful consulting. They are: we establish rapport and trust; we accept and work with people as they are; we think *with* people; we pay attention to the process, not just the product; we resist quick easy answers; we accept who is ultimately in control of the final decision; we clarify expectations, ours and theirs; we communicate in different language modes; we reflect on our practice; we foster district support; we work for organizational change; we use our personal power; and, finally, we have a passion for our work. Collectively, all these things give us the power and impetus to accomplish our goals.

10

IF THERE WAS NOTHING WRONG IN THE WORLD THERE WOULDN'T BE ANYTHING FOR US TO DO.
—*George Bernard Shaw*

DIFFICULT CONSULTING

What makes it challenging?
What should I pay more attention to?

uccessful consulting occurs when two basic conditions are in place: One, you personally pick a colleague with whom you would like to work, and two, they pick you as a colleague with whom they would like to work. You have the potential for the creation of an effective "marriage." Difficult consulting occurs when you do not pick them; your responsibilities include working with them. And they do not pick you; they must work with you to get the help they need. Neither of you has a choice! It is a prearranged "marriage" from the outset. That is difficult consulting. But like a prearranged marriage, you can make it work if you decide to apply the skills you have learned. It is also possible for you to work on this marriage. You will not necessarily like it but it can be done. We know that when one person changes how he or she interacts, it affects the other person in some way.

Just as there are critical factors that influence the success of your consulting efforts, there are also factors that make consulting very difficult and challenging at times. Based on your own experiences and what you have read so far, reflect on what you think makes or might make consulting a difficult challenge for you. Make a list of your top ten factors and compare your notes while reading the pages ahead.

This chapter will discuss many of the factors that make your consulting efforts difficult and challenging at times, but more importantly, it will offer you many ideas about how to work through those difficult times in order to derive more joy from your work as you consult with colleagues.

The following two scenarios are examples of those rare, but stressful, times when consulting is challenging and difficult. This first scenario describes what you might experience as the *consultant* in a problem-solving situation.

Scenario One: A high school teacher seeks your help to implement cooperative learning in his class. While his lecture notes are well organized and comprehensive, students do not seem to appreciate his efforts, and they often "fool around" during direct instruction and when completing in-class assignments. After six weeks of working closely with the teacher to organize students into learning teams and select appropriate cooperative-learning structures for different assignments, he announces that he is no longer going to invest any more of his valuable time in this because, "It is not working. Besides, it is unfair to the top kids who do all the work, while others get a free ride!" After you acknowledge the problem and propose that strategies and structures can be designed to prevent this from happening, he says, "No, I have always believed it would not work, and now I know it does not."

As a peer consultant, what do you do when this happens? What are your options? What would you secretly like to do? What would be the most productive strategy over the long haul? This next scenario describes what a *consultee* might experience that makes the process challenging at times.

Scenario Two: As a middle school teacher, you are concerned because a large segment of your class is what you consider to be poor writers. While you are somewhat concerned about their limited spelling skills, poor handwriting habits, and lack of attention to mechanics, your primary concerns are the lack of paragraph organization and the quality of their thoughts (they can write long paragraphs but their stories lack substance). Without asking you what you already know about teaching writing skills or finding out what you have already tried, your consultant explains how to use a curriculum-based measurement procedure that counts the number of word-increase from one writing sample to the next and how back-up reinforcers can be used to motivate students to write. While these may be great solutions for another problem and another teacher, it is difficult to explain to her that you have major philosophical differences with these approaches. But, then, she never asked!

As a consultee, what do you do when this happens? What would you like to do? As you can see from this scenario, consulting skills are as critical for the consultee as for the consultant, especially if both parties are going to experience success and get their needs met.

The following sections discuss many of the factors that make consulting and communicating very challenging if they are not recognized or addressed early.

YOU HAVE TO WORK WITH PEOPLE WHO ARE NOT LIKE YOU

You are a risk-taker; she wants more assurance. You love to collaborate; he prefers to work alone. You are a dreamer; she is a doer. You rely heavily on your gut instincts; he needs facts and figures. You only want the big picture; she needs the whole picture. The differences abound. How can you possibly work with people who do not think like you and probably do not act like you!

How you respond to these differences will significantly impact your ability to work with colleagues in a consulting relationship. If you can appreciate, value, and celebrate these differences, you can learn to use differences to everyone's advantage and consulting can be a rewarding learning experience.

One of the best strategies for working with people who have different ways of looking at the world and therefore different ways of doing things is to stay focused on your mutual goals. For the most part, educators agree on the goals. We differ primarily on the way or the strategies we select for achieving our goals. For example, we all want students to be good writers (our mutual goal); it is the way that we believe students learn how to be effective writers that may set us apart. We all want students to be motivated and to self-manage their behavior (our mutual goal); it is the way that we motivate students that may set us apart. These differences are not as irresolvable as many people seem to believe. Solutions can be negotiated if you believe there is more than one way to solve a problem. We have much to learn from people who are different from us if we remain open to the experience.

THERE IS LIMITED TIME IN YOUR SCHEDULE TO CONSULT

Even though our personal and professional futures are heavily contingent upon developing supportive work environments, rarely is school time allocated exclusively for this purpose. As a result, isolationism pervades the practice of teaching.

Not only do teachers have insufficient time to complete the tasks already on their plate, but the number of tasks and responsibilities added to their plate seem to increase at the speed of light. The cake decorating scene in the Charlie Chaplin film, "Modern Times" resembles the lives of teachers today. As the conveyer belt speeds up, the cakes go flying by and many end up on the floor. In their haste to keep up with the cakes coming down the belt (students and responsibilities piling up), workers (teachers) spray icing (learning) wherever they can. Unfortunately, teachers sometimes feel that very few "cakes" end up on the shelf intact. As a result, it becomes increasingly more difficult for teachers to be proud of their work.

What can educators do to get more time in their schedules to consult with colleagues? It is best to start with some general principles. First, remember that you only have 24 hours in your day and that is unlikely to change in the near future. Before you put anything new on your schedule, you must take something off. This is not an easy decision to make, but it must be done if you want quality outcomes.

Second, prioritize what really needs to get done and what would be nice to have done. Make an "A" list, a "B" list and a "C" list. Plan your day by starting with the items or objectives on your "A" list, the priority ones, then proceed to the "B" list. If time remains, do items on your "C" list. It helps when you do this to tell yourself repeatedly that *less is more* when you focus on quality rather than quantity.

The third principle to consider is this: Do not own the time problem on your own. It is a school-wide problem. Put the subject of finding time to consult with colleagues on the agenda for discussion when all your colleagues and administrators are present. Think creatively about how to secure more planning time in everyone's schedule. DeBoer & Fister (in press) suggest several ways for educators to get time in their schedules to co-consult, some of which are as follows:

1. Hire substitute teachers for one day every two weeks who float from class to class as needed.

2. Use professional development days for co-consulting.

3. Request that administrators, deans, or counselors cover classes for teachers.

4. Allow students to engage in independent projects or practice activities, while teachers consult with each other in the classroom.

PEOPLE ARE NOT READY FOR CHANGE

Unfortunately, not everybody (sometimes nobody) is ready to change when you are. If you want to help people change, you have to approach people and work with them in their stages of acceptance and not in the one you think they should be. This difference is what makes consulting both challenging and growth-producing.

People move through stages when new ideas are introduced into their life, especially if these ideas are upsetting to their status quo and create dissonance for them. While there are many models that address the stages of change, the one model that seems generic enough to address many different types of change situations is the stages of death by Kubler-Ross (1969). This may seem off-base, but it makes good sense when you consider that when people change their behavior, it often means that they have to give up the past that was often perceived as good, or at least comfortable, and learn new behaviors for the future. During this change process, we often forget to take time for funerals, yet we all know that we need time to grieve before we can move on to renewal.

Kubler-Ross' stages of death are as follows:

- ◆ Denial
- ◆ Anger
- ◆ Bargaining
- ◆ Depression
- ◆ Acceptance

An example of how you might see these stages played out in schools is when teachers are asked to implement a new math program, one that emphasizes problem-based learning and de-emphasizes rote memorization of math facts, formulas, and equations. Initially, some teachers, not all, will be at the stage of *denial*. At this stage, they make statements like, "My program is working just fine. I do not need to change. My student's state test scores support my beliefs." If they continue to experience pressure to change, they will move to the stage of *anger*. (Unfortunately, this one cannot be avoided!) Anger can be expressed covertly or overtly. The former is more difficult to recognize. Anger is often expressed with statements like, "Why should I change? I have always been a good teacher! Besides, they will not give us the time or training to do this, so why should I take on all this responsibility! If they make me do this, I will quit!"

The third stage is *bargaining* and is usually manifested by teachers trying to negotiate how much change they need to make in their program or they try to strike a bargain with either the change agents or themselves by saying, "If I provide proof that my students are performing well on norm-referenced tests and my parents are happy with their progress, then I will only have to add a little problem-based learning to my curriculum every week."

When these first three coping methods fail and there is still pressure (internally or externally imposed) to implement a comprehensive math problem-based curriculum, *depression* follows and is manifested in many ways: isolation, no participation in discussion around the subject, constant complaining about feeling overwhelmed, and being unable to cope with all the demands made on their time. Finally, if sufficient support is provided, a feeling of *acceptance* emerges and teachers start to talk about the inevitable, "How can we do this in a way that I can feel successful with it and it will not hurt my students?"

There are three important things to remember about these stages and change: (1) Everybody goes through these stages when they face what appears to them to be cataclysmic change; they are either fighting to preserve the past or grieving the past; (2) People move through the stages in a sequential order from denial to acceptance and they do not skip over any of the stages; and (3) People rarely move from one stage to another without the support of colleagues. To help people move through the change process, the message must be consistent throughout: We must change, but we will do it together and we will be successful together. Listening and problem solving are key strategies in the process.

FIRST THEY SAY THEY WILL, BUT THEN ...

It is frustrating when you invest your time working on a plan with colleagues but they do not follow through implementing it. This is especially true when you share responsibility for the outcomes. There are many reasons why this might happen, but generally they fall into these seven areas. As you read each, think about what you might do to change things:

1. People may understand the plan that was designed, but be unable to translate that plan into practice in the classroom. Consulting is not unlike a pull-out program where it is difficult to transfer information from one setting to another. It may be that the person is finding it hard to get started because the first step of implementation is unclear.

2. The plan that was designed was never theirs in the first place; it was our plan for them, so they lack ownership.

3. People do not really believe that it is in their best interests to implement the plan. Any plan must meet the teachers' needs as well as the students' needs.

4. People have other pressures and demands on their time, so priorities have changed. The timelines for implementation need to be reset.

5. The plan that was designed seemed right at the time but as it was being implemented, new information surfaced and, as a result, a different action plan was deemed necessary.

6. No clear time lines were set during problem solving as to what would be done when. What you assumed is not what they assumed.

7. It was never their need to meet with you to plan a program. It was someone else's need for this to happen—a mandate or an edict was issued. If the process was not voluntary, lack of follow through may be the only way for the person to keep his or her personal power and self-respect. The old adage applies: You can lead a horse to water but you cannot make him drink. (But it is also true that if you can salt his oats or sweeten the water, you may have a chance.) As a peer consultant, you have no direct power to influence change so you have to learn to use your personal power. (Chapter 9 discussed strategies for developing personal power.)

It is also possible that the person with whom you are working is resistant for reasons that are not clearly obvious to you or for reasons that you find difficult to support. Try to remember that resistance is a primarily a needs issue; if you can figure out their needs, you can probably influence them.

CONSULTEES ARE OFTEN UNAWARE OF THEIR ROLE IN THE PROCESS

It is ironic that, if any training is done, all the emphasis is placed on training people who will function in the role of the consultant but little emphasis is placed on helping consultees understand their roles and responsibilities in the process. The success of consulting efforts is the responsibility of both the consultee and the consultant. Both need to have ownership in the process and be committed to making the process work. Furthermore, if both parties are to play reciprocal roles, both need to be involved in the following activities:

- Mutually designing a problem-solving structure.
- Clarifying personal needs that must be addressed during the process.
- Deciding which interactive approach is best.
- Clarifying goals, objectives, and expectations for the meeting.
- Listening and communicating effectively.
- Gathering and organizing relevant assessment data.
- Recognizing interpersonal styles.
- Learning how to provide feedback.
- Saying "no" without feeling guilty or resistant.
- Managing differences of opinion on issues or strategies.

The probability of success doubles when these decisions are understood, addressed, and designed collaboratively.

WHAT THEY THINK YOUR ROLE IS, DIFFERS FROM YOUR PERCEPTION OF IT

Do the following scenes seem familiar to you? They think your role is to supply them with materials to implement a program or additional materials for students who need extra help; you think your role is to alert them as to particular materials and resources that are available for the problems they face. They think your role is to work directly with students in the classroom; you think your role is to design strategies with them that they will implement on their own. They think your role is to assess learning and/or behavioral problems and determine an appropriate label (reading disabled, Chapter One, ESL, learning disabled, etc.); you think your role is to assess how curriculum and classroom instruction can be enhanced or adapted to meet individual needs during whole-class instruction. They think your role is to provide answers to all their questions; you think your role is to facilitate their finding their own answers to their problems.

They expect you to have answers for their complex problems before you fully understand the problem; you expect them to provide a clear picture of the problem and their feelings about it before you mutually discuss options. These differences in role expectations can be frustrating and confusing for all the parties involved.

Unfortunately, some consultants really do believe that it is their job to provide answers for other people and, in some situations, consultants often are expected to label students by categories for instruction. As a result, these practices keep colleagues dependent on them. An important role of a consultant is to help people design a process for assessing and solving their own problems in the future.

When consultants get strong messages from consultees that they are expected to supply them with answers or determine pathology, they have to work hard not to get caught in the trap. If you try to fulfill someone else's image of an effective consultant, you may suffer from the "Imposter Syndrome" (I am not what people think I am). It is a heavy burden to be so wise all the time and to be responsible for putting labels on students that may be with them all the days of their lives. To avoid the trap, very early in the process (at the entry level), discuss and clarify roles so that there are not major disappointments and frustration later.

DIFFERENTIATING A CONSULTING ISSUE FROM AN ADMINISTRATIVE ISSUE

One area that causes considerable stress for many people who find themselves in the role of a peer consultant is determining when a situation is a consulting issue and when it is an administrative issue. Typically they are faced with these three questions:

1. When, and in what kinds of problems, do I get involved as a peer consultant, and when is it clearly an administrative problem?

2. If I am involved in a difficult situation, how do I honestly and courageously bow out and when should I turn it over to an administrator?

3. If I do turn a problem over to an administrator, how do I make this transfer without damaging trust?

What follows are guidelines for approaching these issues, not absolute rules for all times and all situations. The first question can be addressed by asking yourself two things: First, was the request for consultation self-initiated? If so, it is generally appropriate to get involved. Second, what are your parameters for the types of problems you will discuss with colleagues? This is your decision to make. Some issues are very appropriate: classroom instruction, assessment and monitoring strategies, or classroom management. Other issues are not appropriate: problems with other teachers, providing direct support to students, or problems with the administration.

The following scenario is one you may always want to avoid or at least give considerable thought to prior to getting involved:

◆ A principal requests your help to "fix" an ineffective teacher in the school. The principal tells you that she does not have the expertise on this specific area to address the problem. She now turns the problem over to you because you are considered to have the expertise that is needed.

What is a peer consultant to do? First of all, remember that people do not change their behavior unless they feel a need to change—in this case, "get fixed." So, the first question you ask your administrator before plunging in (after being flattered that she picked you for this tough job) is, "Does the teacher know that he or she has a problem?" Then, "Does he or she know that you are asking me to work with him or her, and why?" If the answer is "no" to either of these questions, the ground work has definitely not been laid for you to get involved. The principal must discuss the issues with the teacher prior to your entry. If he or she does not, a dyslexic in a speed-reading contest has a better chance of succeeding than you do.

It is helpful to view this scenario from the context of direct and indirect power. An administrator has direct power for implementing (or insisting on) change. A peer consultant has only indirect power for influencing change. It is an administrator's responsibility to assure that quality education is available for all students in the school. As a peer consultant, you can only assist in this process, not demand it; you can only design and monitor programs with a teacher, not supervise them.

If and when you do choose to get involved in a difficult change process at the request of an administrator, your role as a peer consultant must be clarified very early with the consultee. It is critical that you position yourself on the teacher's side against the problem. You may need to begin the conversation by saying something like this before you agree to the challenge: "Before we proceed, I would appreciate you telling me why you think we are meeting." It is not unusual for a teacher to respond in a situation like this with, "Because the principal thinks I have a problem!" It now needs to be determined if the consultee chooses to respond to the administrative concern, not your concern! The teacher may want to do something, anything, to get the principal off his or her case.

This next scene addresses getting out of a difficult situation and maintaining trust:

  ◆ A teacher fails to follow through, week after week, on a
     mutually designed plan. You have diligently followed up on
     a mutually agreed upon schedule trying to remove the bar-
     riers to implementation.

What is a peer consultant to do? Following documented and systematic attempts to provide the necessary support, you must now confront (this does not mean attack!) the consultee with *your* problem. Your statement could sound something like this:

  ◆ "We have been discussing this problem for eight weeks and
     I am not seeing any implementation of our action plan. How
     do you see us working this out?"

If there is no response or change in behavior, you may need to be a little more assertive (this is not to be confused with aggressive, although emotionally you want to attack him or her at this point):

  ◆ "We have been struggling with this plan for 12 weeks and
     we do not seem to be able to work this problem out. The
     reasons are unimportant to me at this point. But we do need

to make some changes as I can no longer continue to invest my time without some action on your part. Do we need to involve another colleague who may be able to offer some additional ideas about where we can go from here?"

If you are in the precarious position of sharing responsibility and accountability for the implementation of a program, as is often the case for special education and other support services, you may want to go one step further before you exit stage left:

♦ "Because we do not seem to be able to reach agreement on timelines for implementing this program, I can no longer invest my time without some action on your part. I think we need to involve the principal to see if she can offer some ideas about where we can go from here. When would you like to do this?"

The choices are obvious and the responsibility for the direction to be taken is placed squarely on the consultee's shoulders. If he or she chooses not to invest time or energy in solving the problem, you must put it in the hands of the administrator. As a peer consultant, you have no power to make consultees do what you believe to be in the best interests of students (or force compliance to an Individual Education Plan [IEP] if you are a special education teacher). First, try all your sources of personal power. Then, if necessary, diplomatically involve your administrator.

If you want to develop and maintain trust, it is always good practice, to be tenaciously honest and upfront with a colleague before turning the problem over to an administrator. People may not always agree with you and your choices, but they will respect your integrity. I-statements are an invaluable technique to use in these situations because they surface the problem and provide colleagues with choices. I-statements are discussed in detail in Chapter 5.

SOMETIMES YOU HAVE TO WORK WITH "THE HARD-CORE UNINFORMED" TYPE

As you try to make consulting a school-wide practice because of its benefits to teachers and subsequently to students, you eventually have to work with difficult people just as you have to work with students who are difficult. They are there whether we like it or not. The author has had several personal experiences with this difficult challenge. It helps to reframe it as a learning opportunity. The author's first job as a consulting teacher was in 1972-73. The entire experience seemed to be a disaster at the time; almost everything that could go wrong, did! This happened, in part, because teachers were not involved in designing the process. It was not a voluntary interaction for either the consultant or the consultee. As a result of many repeated challenges, she identified these core groups of people with whom she worked:

- The Hard-Core Uninformed
- The Guilt-Ridden
- The Self-Starters

The *Hard-Core Uninformed* group seemed at the time to be about 50-60% of the teachers in the district (an erroneous belief, of course). They could be identified easily because of their defensive and discouraging remarks:

- "I have already tried it. It does not work!"
- "You surely do not believe that is possible in a class of 30, do you?"
- "That sounds good in theory, but it will not work with this kid."

It was easy to blame all the failures on these teachers. They appeared to be resistant to any suggestions or ideas that were offered to solve the problems that they complained about. But as time passed, and as she listened to this group again and again, it became increasingly obvious that they had their own stories to tell. It became clearer to her that many of these teachers had been sincere, dedicated individuals at one time, but received little support or encouragement for their efforts. After years of trying to cope with the daily demands of teaching, they now appeared negative, uncooperative, and jaded. The author eventually learned, as a result of her persistence, that you can work with them and, over time, effect change.

The *Guilt-Ridden* were teachers who were very relieved when it appeared that the student owned the problem, that it was an inside-the-head problem and not, in any way, related to instruction, curriculum, or classroom environment. They loved labels such as lazy, unmotivated, slow learner, mild dyslexia, learning disabled, severe memory problem, or visual discrimination deficit. Labels imply that there is something wrong with the student's attitude or brain. The Guilt-Ridden needed to believe that they were not at fault. However, they also had their strengths: they knew in their solar plexus that student achievement was their responsibility and they wanted to do the right thing.

The *Self-Starters* were her joy and survival. They were the people who provided early success and sold the benefits of consulting to others. You recognize Self-Starters because they have already tried several strategies in their attempts to solve a problem. The role of a peer consultant is clearly evident; you think with them and provide support for their efforts at change.

To experience success, it is best to start with people who have the highest probability of profiting from cooperative efforts—the Self-Starters—then proceed to the group who have the second highest probability, and so on. The reason for this is obvious: if you do not do yourself a big favor by getting some early successes, you will run out of fuel. It is a truism that you cannot help others unless you take care of yourself. Successes are like money in the bank; they motivate you to continue through more difficult times.

SOME PEOPLE REFUSE TO WORK WITH COLLEAGUES

There are individuals in every school or district who will either hesitate or refuse to work with you, no matter how wonderful you or your colleagues are. Do not personalize this! There are a number of reasons to explain this that have little or nothing to do with you personally. For example:

♦ Requesting help may be perceived as an admission of inadequacy to oneself and others, and this is too difficult for them to acknowledge.

♦ There may be anxiety about confidentiality. Developing trust takes more time for them and needs to be constantly earned.

♦ Many fear that if they ask a lot of questions, they will be perceived as incompetent. Their history tells them that teachers are supposed to have answers, not questions.

♦ There may be a perception, frequently based on reality, that it takes too much time to consult with colleagues. They would rather go it alone.

♦ The time required to work together may not be perceived as worth the effort—a personal decision.

♦ Some people fear that they will be too exposed and possibly evaluated if they share their practices with colleagues. This fear can be both personal and professional.

♦ They perceive you, for whatever reasons, as an outsider who is not worthy of either their time or trust.

♦ Some people have a generalized fear of change because of some unknown factor. For example, they may not want to upset the status quo even if present conditions are not satisfactory, or they may think it is better to stick with the devil you know than risk the one you could get.

At this point, you may want to reread each item and think about what you might need to do to remove each barrier in regards to your particular situation.

YOU MIGHT HAVE TO DEAL WITH ANGRY PEOPLE

Why do some people lose their temper and verbally attack others? Generally, because it works for them, at least on the surface. Angry outbursts are intimidating to most of us. As a result, we tend to back off and let angry people have their own way, at least for the moment. When we are attacked by an angry person, it always seems to happen without warning and for no apparent reason. And it *never* feels good!

Whenever we are under attack, our body reacts physiologically by preparing to engage in a fight-or-flight response. Our whole system enters a state of hyperactivism in which our heart races, our body temperature rises, and our oxygen consumption increases. All of these symptoms signal that we are under stress and are feeling a strong urge to either counterattack or flee. Because neither option is socially appropriate (or solves the problem), we have to muster up all of our resources to respond in a rational and dignified manner as well as act in a manner that yields productive outcomes.

An additional factor that further complicates the situation is that while you are trying to pull yourself together, you cannot be sure that the angry person is functioning rationally either, so anything you say or do is likely to be misconstrued. Therefore, a guideline during these difficult times is to move slowly and evaluate all your options, rather than engage in a knee-jerk reaction and make matters worse than they already are.

There are a number of reasons why people might attack others in anger. One, mentioned earlier, is that they have learned to react this way. That learning occurred as a result of repeated reinforcement when others reacted as they did and gave them what they wanted. A second reason may be that the situation in which they find themselves is similar to a previous situation that caused them high stress. As a result, they react with angry outbursts without think-ing—a conditioned response. A third reason may be that when people are under prolonged stress as a result of not getting their needs met, the current situation becomes the straw that breaks the camel's back. In frustration, they unfairly strike out. A fourth reason is that some people unconsciously use anger as a defensive tactic to cope with their fears and/or sense of helplessness. Having said all this, it is also true that there are a few individuals in our universe (and we can probably name some immediately) who use anger in conscious and deliberate ways to manipulate others. As you well know, these individuals can be very difficult to work with.

Dealing with angry people is chiefly a matter of helping them regain self-control. Your ability to respond to anger by perceiving it accurately (in other words, what is their real need?) and reacting to it calmly under emotionally-charged circumstances takes some thought. Here are some guidelines for dealing with anger:

◆ Give angry people time to get calmed down. You cannot expect them to appreciate your wonderful words of wisdom when they are exploding. Allow them sufficient time to dissipate some of the anger. Allow and even help them express their feelings by saying, "Tell me more," "What else?" or "Wow! Bummer! No kidding!" Until they feel that you have listened, your logic and explanations are futile. It is not unusual for angry people, when they suddenly realize what they are doing, to automatically calm down. During this entire period, try to stay calm or at least look calm. If their self-imposed spell seems to be endless (from your vantage point), you may have to take action by suddenly and unexpectedly standing up (or sitting down if you are standing), raising your voice slightly to catch their attention, and saying things such as, "Wait a minute!" or "Stop," or "Susan . . . ." Be as dramatic as you need to be. Using the person's name can be very calming if it is done right. Watch your tone of voice. Do not sound controlling or disapproving. Whatever you do, do not argue or respond to the issues under discussion. This will only prolong or escalate their anger.

◆ Show sincere interest in the problem and the person by actively listening. Let them know that you understand how important this issue is to them and that you want to discuss it further, but not in this way. You may have to send this message again and again in a number of ways before they hear it. Accept the person's right to be angry, even when you do not agree with the reasons, by saying something such as, "If I were in your position, I might feel the same way. What role do you want me to play?" Allow people the freedom of being wrong, that is, of course, from your point of view. Try to capture their message and, when appropriate, reflect their feelings. This also has a calming effect. People feel better when they know that others understand how it must feel for them.

◆ Avoid a head-on fight, but also let them know you cannot be bulldozed by their anger. Because anger usually works for them, try to break this pattern by speaking up for yourself honestly and openly. Maintain eye contact when appropriate. Speak from your point of view by consistently using assertive I-statements (see Chapter 5) by saying something such as, "I feel nervous when I am perceived as the enemy because my need is to help." In this way, you avoid telling them what to do or whether you think they are right or wrong; you only communicate how it seems to you.

◆ Look for areas of common interest or agreement. If you cannot agree with their ideas, try to agree with their right to be concerned about the problem. Genuinely commend them for their strong commitment to finding a solution to the problem by saying something such as, "Sounds like you really want to resolve this."

◆ Communicate in a supportive manner by saying something such as, "Sounds like you have had a difficult time." Good communication adds to everyone's pleasure. Be ready to be friendly when the storm has passed. This will earn their respect.

AVOIDING JUDGMENTS

To fully understand and feel how destructive judging can be, recall a situation that happened to you recently in which you were the recipient of a negative judgment. You probably felt surprised, indignant, belittled, defensive, and/or angry. You probably continue to avoid your judge to this day by always having excuses for not being able to get together. No one likes to feel judged by others. Besides, we already have a critical judge—ourselves. We do not need another judge; we need supportive colleagues.

Not making judgments about people may be the greatest human challenge we face when we work with colleagues. Judgments are so easy to make and we often make them quickly and unconsciously. Passing judgment on others is destructive of collegial relationships. It damages trust. It inhibits colleagues from taking risks to openly discuss their problems and dreams as well as their feelings about them. It is particularly devastating to colleagues who either lack personal confidence or lack the necessary information and skills to change.

Even when we are aware that we are "gifted" at passing judgments, it is difficult to give up, perhaps because when we complain, or behave indignantly about people's behavior, it allows us to feel "just a little bit superior" (John Richards, personal communication, 1987). For a brief moment in time, we feel more competent than they are. (And just between you and me, once in a while it feels good to feel just a little bit superior.) This good feeling, unfortunately, reinforces and maintains our judging behavior.

There are many ways in which we pass judgments on others or they pass judgments on us. Often they occur at a nonverbal level. For example, even though we do not make these statements aloud, people sense when we are thinking, "I cannot believe he did that!" or "How did she get a teaching license!" Our facial expressions and body language are windows to our thoughts. Our tone of voice (pitch and intonation) and timing contain nonverbal messages. In fact, they are thought to carry better than 90% of the message. It is not what we say, it is the way we say it that gets us in trouble.

A second way that we pass judgments is by the content of the questions we ask. What we say is often not what we mean, so self-monitor if you do not want to offend others. Judging questions can sound like this:

- "Why do you emphasize grammar during writing instruction?"
- "What strategies have you already tried to solve this problem?"

These questions can leave people with a "should feeling"—they should not emphasize grammar, or they should have tried something already.

A third way we pass judgments is by the statements we make. Again, these are often made in innocence and stated with kindness. Statements can either imply approval and, in their absence, disapproval or a mild case of incompetence. Consider these statements:

- ◆ "Good for you! You did a great job of implementing a difficult strategy."
- ◆ "That was a good try!"
- ◆ "I think I know what needs to be done here."
- ◆ "Do not worry, I will be around to help you if you get stuck."
- ◆ "I would like to involve others. You are going to need a lot of help with this."

Giving compliments like, "That was a great job you did with Adam," feels good, but it is risky business. As a colleague, you need to stick with feedback that is neutral like, "You positively reinforced Adam's behavior four times during this period. He responded positively by completing more work." Offering help, as is indicated in the last three statements above, when it is not requested is also risky. It can imply superiority and dependence which, of course, is not a winning strategy.

Not making judgments about people does not mean that you agree with them or their behavior. It simply means that you accept their right to make decisions that differ from yours. Your role, if you disagree, is to try to influence them by presenting your own points-of-view in a convincing manner. Your communication skills and questioning techniques will determine your success with this.

Be Tenacious About Using Win/Win Strategies

When dealing with tough people and tough situations, as will likely be the case at some point when working with people in organizations, consistently use Win/Win strategies. These strategies are rarely easy to use, so you must remain diligent at all times. Win/Win strategies are designed explicitly to produce wise outcomes in an efficient and amicable manner. The overall picture is one of mutual gain. Unfortunately, we live in a society pervaded by potential Win/Lose situations in which there is competition for getting our needs met or being right at the expense of others. As unbelievable as it may seem to us near perfect creatures, there are actually people out there who are willing to sacrifice themselves to a Lose/Lose situation. They are prepared to expend valuable energy on getting even or playing revenge games. In successful consulting, Win/Win strategies are always the goal. The focus is on defeating the problem, not other people.

Win/Win strategies, as described by Fisher & Ury (1981), have four basic elements that are integral parts of negotiating. They are, without question, integral parts of consulting as well. They are:

1. Separate the person from the problem.

2. Focus on mutual interests, not opposing positions.

3. Collaboratively generate several options prior to making decisions.

4. Base final decisions on objective criteria, not on who is the most tenacious.

Each of these elements needs to be understood and applied when consulting and communicating with colleagues. If you take time to apply them, the strategies will yield dramatic results, often immediately.

Separate the person from the problem

Every effort must be made to separate the person from the problem. In other words, avoid treating the person and the problem as one. We all know how difficult this is to do at times, but to consult successfully, we must view ourselves as working together on the same side against a problem. We jointly attack a mutual problem, not each other.

Failure to work with others sensitively as fellow human beings capable of strong emotions and overreactions can be disastrous. People often hold radically different views about issues like student motivation, how children learn to read, and grading. Unfortunately, strong emotions, first initiated by the problem, become entangled with the person. This entanglement only serves to complicate the situation and make matters worse.

During those times when people do become enmeshed with the problem, the situation can be improved by increasing the amount of time for communication, clarifying misconceptions, and exploring the feelings behind the stated problem. This can be done by actively listening and openly acknowledging what the other person is saying. The most persuasive thing you can do is to let a person know you have heard him or her and that you accept his or her perception of the problem. Again, remember that acceptance does not mean that you agree. It only means that you accept another person's right to think differently.

Focus on mutual interests

When planning and problem solving, attention should be focused on mutual interests and mutual gains, not on predetermined, hard-lined positions. People's interests (needs and concerns) are what causes them to assume a certain position, so try to search out their interests rather than argue with them about their position on an issue. Here is an example of a position: A colleague arrives at a student conference and assumes a firm position on a student's placement, either in or out of a special program, prior to any discussion regarding what is best for the student.

When we assume certain positions on issues and then subsequently attempt to defend them through argument, several negative consequences can occur: (1) we tend to lock ourselves into positions we then are forced to defend, (2) our egos become enmeshed with our positions so that a new interest surfaces—saving face, (3) more time is devoted to positional bargaining and less to the underlying needs or concerns of both parties, and (4) arguing over positions endangers the trust that is established or needs to be developed among people.

Generate several options together

A variety of options should be generated before any decision is made. The group brain via brainstorming techniques is an invaluable resource for creating alternatives that advance mutual interests and reconcile differences. Fisher & Ury (1981) have identified four major obstacles that invariably inhibit the creation of an abundance of options: (1) premature judgment or criticism of a potential solution, thereby inhibiting creativity, (2) a search for the one best solution early in the process so as to decrease the pain of decision making when too many alternatives are available, (3) the assumption of a "fixed pie," that is, people believe there is a limited amount of anything available and, as a result, decisions are either/or in nature, and (4) the belief that a problem is someone else's to solve, rather than seeing problems as a shared concern for all parties to resolve collaboratively.

When the focus is on mutual needs and interests, to everyone's delight, creative solutions often are found. Here is an example: A colleague wants a student removed from the classroom (a position). You believe it is in the student's best interest to remain with his peers in the classroom (also a position). During problem solving, mutual interests are discussed: The teacher wants the student to remain on-task for a longer duration without disturbing other students. You also want the student to attend to his or her own affairs and get his or her work completed, but you also want him or her to remain with peers who can provide appropriate models and reinforcement. By focusing on your mutual interests—the student's success—a time management strategy is designed for the student that is supported by both of you.

Base final decisions on objective criteria

It must be recognized that no matter how well you have attempted to address mutual interests, there are those difficult times when interests conflict and appear to be irreconcilable. During these difficult times, the efficacy of any final decision should be evaluated using some ethical, fair standards such as exemplary models, research findings, third party examples, and/or expert judgment. No decision should be accepted because of pressure or as a result of who has the strongest will. If it is, the results are only temporary at best and both parties lose. Win/Win strategies must be used if permanent, binding solutions to problems are to emerge. (Anyone interested in studying the concept of Win/Win strategies in greater depth is strongly encouraged to read Fisher & Ury's excellent book, *Getting To Yes: Negotiating Agreement Without Giving In.*)

YOU NEED STRATEGIES FOR MANAGING RESISTANCE

If your role in the school is that of a consulting teacher, you are automatically in the role of a change agent. As a change agent, you should expect resistance from at least 80-85% of the people, for different reasons and at different times. It helps to view resistance or rejection as a necessary step on the road to acceptance. Each rejection simply means you are moving closer to your goal. When you think about it, we have all rejected new ideas when they are first brought to our attention, so we need to accept it as a natural course of events and the first step to "yes." In fact, the response "no" only means "No, for now." As our knowledge and skills increase, we will feel more comfortable with the idea and our resistance dissipates.

People resist change for any number of reasons: fear of an unknown entity; a need to protect their turf; a belief that time-honored practices should be held sacrosanct; lack of trust in the change agent or the system; lack of clarity as to the purpose and benefits of a proposed change; and/or confusion about how to implement it. While it is important to understand the source and nature of resistance, it is equally important to know how to manage it. Before we discuss strategies, here are some thoughts to keep in mind when you experience resistance:

♦ Resistance is your problem, not theirs.

♦ Resistance is probably something you created when you raised the issue. (They were probably delightful, happy people until you came into their lives and suggested a possible change.)

♦ People do not resist change; they resist uncertainty. Security, derived from predictable environments, is a high priority for most of us. (We all learned this in Psychology 101.)

♦ People usually do not resist change; they resist being changed by others and on someone else's timeline.

There are several excellent strategies for managing resistance. What follows is a discussion of some of the best:

♦ *Change resistance by accepting it.* Get on their side against the problem. Express interest and curiosity in any objections that are raised by saying, "Tell me more," or asking "What else?" Then honor their concerns by paraphrasing their objections. This communicates that you are an astute, caring person who is worthy of being heard. Until you actively listen, they cannot hear. Often the temptation is to push harder with more of the same arguments and rationale which only stiffens their resistance.

♦ *Look for areas of agreement.* You must find something to which you can agree and feel comfortable with. If you cannot agree with an idea, you probably can agree with their feelings, given their frame of reference. Another option is to agree with a small statement or phrase that they made by acknowledging it. For example, "I totally agree; we have to be practical about this." It is much easier to move from agreement to agreement then from disagreement to agreement. It seems that on psychological issues the most important thing to some people is not to be logical, but to be right. Wars are waged on this central issue. Some people will do almost anything to sustain the belief that they are right. Therefore, find something that they are right about and move on to the next step.

◆ *Involve critical stakeholders in the planning.* Have those people most affected by the change participate in problem finding then developing possible solutions. People are willing to expend time and energy on implementing *their* decisions.

◆ *Identify the problems before they do.* It is often better if the problems are surfaced by you, especially if you can express your concerns about how they might feel. Make statements like, "If I were in your position, this is how I might be feeling," or "If I were in your position, this is what I probably would be thinking."

◆ *Ask what it would take to convince them that the proposed change is in their best interests.* This takes the pressure off you and opens things up for new information. Make statements like, "What needs to happen for you to be convinced . . . ?" If you listen with real interest and curiosity, they will tell you exactly how to do it and gain their support.

◆ *Play the devil's advocate.* You can do this by saying something like, "If I were in your position, I would think or feel exactly like you. Now if you were in my position, what would you do?" You may now have new information to work with.

Whatever strategies you use for managing resistance, remember that none of them will be effective unless you use them with sincerity and a real desire to understand others' interests. Strategies used carelessly and without concern for others can create a backlash and make things worse. Proceed with caution and, above all, be authentic.

THE MESSAGE

There are many conditions and situations that make consulting difficult and challenging: working with difficult and sometimes angry people; lacking experience with tough situations; not having enough time for consulting; colleagues not open to change; limited follow through after a commitment has been made; insufficient training for difficult new situations; conflicting expectations about your role; differentiating between a consulting issue and an administrative issue; colleagues refusing to work together; avoiding judgments; always using Win/Win strategies; and developing strategies for managing resistance. As difficult as it may seem, all of these challenges can become learning opportunities if you decide to apply the skills and knowledge discussed throughout this book.

While consulting is always great fun when it works for everyone involved, we do not always get what we want. It helps, during difficult times to remember the wise words of Ralph Waldo Emerson, "Do what you will, summer will have its flies."

" . . . AND SO THERE AIN'T NOTHING MORE TO WRITE ABOUT, AND I AM ROTTEN GLAD OF IT, BECAUSE IF I'D A KNOWED WHAT A TROUBLE IT WAS TO MAKE A BOOK I WOULDN'T A TACKLED IT AND AIN'T AGOING TO NO MORE."

—MARK TWAIN
in the conclusion to
The Adventures of Huckleberry Finn

APPENDIX A

Listening: A Self-Evaluation

As you read through each item, reflect on your listening skills, then select one skill that you believe would significantly improve your ability to listen effectively. Visualize yourself using the skill with a colleague, then go practice it at least 25 times in the next three weeks until it becomes a habit. Return to this list and pick another one to practice.

_____ 1. Am I prepared physically to listen (e.g., body orientation, fully facing)?

_____ 2. Am I comfortably maintaining eye contact?

_____ 3. Have I made the commitment to listen?

_____ 4. Am I mentally open to this person?

_____ 5. Am I listening for the message (emotions), not just to the words?

_____ 6. Am I monitoring my biases and prejudices?

_____ 7. Am I constantly monitoring my attention?

_____ 8. Am I monitoring my interruptions?

_____ 9. Am I listening from the speaker's point of view?

_____ 10. Am I being empathic?

_____ 11. Am I listening with my purpose in mind?

_____ 12. Am I making value judgments?

_____ 13. Am I hearing what is not being said?

_____ 14. Am I monitoring my facial expressions?

_____ 15. Am I monitoring my body language?

_____ 16. Am I monitoring their facial expressions?

_____ 17. Am I monitoring their body language?

_____ 18. Am I resisting distractions?

_____ 19. Am I using minimum encouragers?

_____ 20. Am I paraphrasing when it seems appropriate?

_____ 21. Am I clarifying when it is necessary and appropriate?

_____ 22. Am I checking perceptions when it is appropriate?

_____ 23. Am I reflecting feelings when it is appropriate?

_____ 24. Am I summarizing when it is appropriate?

APPENDIX B

Communicating: A Self-Evaluation

As you read through each item, reflect on your listening skills, then select one skill that you believe would significantly improve your ability to listen effectively. Visualize yourself using the skill with a colleague, then go practice it at least 25 times in the next three weeks until it becomes a habit. Return to this list and pick another one to practice.

_____ 1. Do I build rapport by communicating a caring attitude?

_____ 2. Do I value my listener?

_____ 3. Do I check in with my listener frequently?

_____ 4. Do I involve my listener?

_____ 5. Do I make what I say relevant to their lives?

_____ 6. Do I self-disclose when appropriate?

_____ 7. Do I encourage feedback by asking them to paraphrase and reflect occasionally?

_____ 8. Do I match my pace to the person or situation?

_____ 9. Do I monitor my nonverbal language (e.g., voice tone, body language, facial expressions, eye contact)?

_____ 10. Do I monitor their nonverbal language (e.g., voice tone, body language, facial expressions, eye contact)?

_____ 11. Do I check their frame of reference?

_____ 12. Do I openly communicate my assumptions and intentions?

_____ 13. Do I make my verbal and nonverbal language congruent?

_____ 14. Do I describe situations in precise, behavioral terms devoid of judgments and interpretations?

_____ 15. Do I own my messages by speaking in the first person (e.g., I and my)?

_____16. Do I restate when appropriate and when the information is important?

_____17. Do I communicate using all styles: verbal, visual, and haptic?

_____18. Do I avoid jargon, abbreviated terms, and acronyms?

_____19. Do I monitor my use of questions?

_____20. Do I use open and closed questions appropriately?

_____21. Do I use direct and indirect questions appropriately?

_____22. Do I avoid why questions?

_____23. Do I send I-messages when I need to?

_____24. Do I always avoid You-messages?

APPENDIX C

What is My Style? What is Your Style?

Our interpersonal styles indicate our strengths and our preferences. Fortunately, there is no one best style. The following inventory can provide you with a small glimpse of your preferred style. To determine your style, check (✓) the one item on each line that best describes you as you see yourself. Total the number of checks in each column and enter the number below.

	a		b		c		d	
1. My primary need is to:	Have a position of influence.		Get recognition for my work.		Have my work appreciated.		Have predictability in my work.	
2. I enjoy work that:	Allows me independent decisions.		Has flexibility and variety.		Involves other colleagues.		Is technical and clearly defined.	
3. I like to work with colleagues who are:	Productive and decisive.		Intense and enthusiastic.		Committed and dependable.		Thorough and sensitive to details.	
4. I prefer work that involves:	Pragmatic and efficient results.		New approaches and different ideas.		A friendly work environment.		A search for the right solution.	
5. If and when I can, I avoid:	Long debates.		Detailed analysis of things.		Conflict with colleagues.		Disorganized environments.	
6. My personal strengths are:	Leading and decision making.		Motivating and communicating.		Listening and acknowledging.		Reasoning and debating the facts.	
7. When time is of the essence, I:	Make a tentative plan and move on it.		Push timelines to the limit.		Am willing to work extra hours.		Set priorities and follow the plan.	
8. In social settings, I:	Initiate conversations.		Am gregarious and fun loving.		Am the listener in the group.		Appear to be serious and quiet.	
9. The work I do allows me:	The power to change people.		Freedom and flexibility.		Opportunities to work with people.		To be accurate and comprehensive.	
10. Colleagues describe me as:	Self-confident and determined.		Energetic and entertaining.		Facilitating and supporting.		Disciplined, orderly, and pensive.	
11. My decisions are generally:	Realistic and decisive.		Creative and evolving.		Respectful of people's needs.		Systematic and abstract.	
12. I dislike:	Losing control.		Boring work.		Frequent change.		Guesswork.	
Style and Total								

Your highest score indicates your primary style, your next highest is your secondary style, your third highest is your tertiary style, and your lowest score indicates the style you are least likely to use or understand in others. If your highest score is in column *a*, you prefer an ***Achiever*** style. If your highest score is in column *b*, you prefer a ***Persuader*** style. If your highest score is in column *c*, you prefer a ***Supporter*** style. If your highest score is in column *d*, you prefer an ***Analyst*** style. For more valid and reliable measures of your interpersonal style, see the commercially available inventories that are listed in Appendix D. Detailed information on your preferred style and strategies for working successfully with colleagues are presented in Chapters 6, 7, and 8 of this book.

APPENDIX D
Interpersonal Style Inventories

There are several interpersonal style inventories that can provide you with a valid and reliable measure of your preferred behavioral style. Here are a few of them:

Interpersonal Style Questionnaire
by Anita DeBoer
Sopris West Educational Services
4093 Specialty Place, Longmont, CO 80504
(800) 547-6747

Leadership Opinion Questionnaire
by Edwin Fleishman
London House/S.R.A.
9701 West Higgins Rd., Rosemont, IL 60018
(800) 237-7685

Learning Style Inventory
by David A. Kolb
McBer & Company
116 Huntington Ave. Boston, MA 02116
(617) 425-4500

Myers-Briggs Type Indicator
by Isabel Myers & Katheryn Briggs
Consulting Psychologists Press
3803 E. Bayshore Rd., Palo Alto, CA 94303
(415) 969-8901

Personal Profile Systems
by John Geier & Michael O'Connor
Performax Systems International, Inc.
14502 West 105th St., Lenexa, KA 66215
(800) 633-5613

Alpert, J.L. & Meyers, J. (Eds.). (1983). *Training in consultation: Perspectives from mental health, behavioral, and organizational consultation.* Springfield, IL: Thomas.

Bandler, R. & Grinder, J. (1975). *The structure of magic I.* Palo Alto, CA: Science and Behavior Books.

Benjamin, A. (1981). *The helping interview.* Geneva, IL: Houghton Mifflin.

Bergen, J.R. (1977). *Behavioral consultation.* Columbus, OH: Merrill.

Caplan, G. (1970). *The theory and practice of mental health consultation.* New York: Basic Books.

Chalfant, J.C., Pysh, M. V. D., & Moultrie, R. (1979). Teacher assistance teams: A model for within-building problem solving. *Learning Disability Quarterly, 2*; 85-96.

Cohen, H. (1980). *You can negotiate anything.* New York: Bantam.

Conoley, J.C. (1981). Advocacy consultation: Promises and problems. In J.C. Conoley (Ed.), *Consultation in the schools.* (pp. 157-178). New York: Academic Press.

Conoley, J.C. & Conoley, C.W. (1982). *School consultation: A guide to practice and training.* New York: Pergamon Press.

Covey, S.R. (1989). *The seven habits of highly effective people.* New York: Simon and Schuster.

DeBoer, A. & Fister, S. (in press). *Strategies & tools for collaborative teaching.* Longmont, CO: Sopris West.

Fisher, R. & Brown, S. (1988). *Getting together: Building relationships as we negotiate.* New York: Penguin.

Fisher, R. & Ury, W. (1981). *Getting to yes: Negotiating agreement without giving in.* New York: Penguin.

Friend, M. & Cook, L. (1992). *Interactions: Collaboration skills for school professionals.* New York: Longman.

Fullan, M. & Hargreaves, A. (1991). *What's worth fighting for? Working together for your school.* Toronto: Ontario Public School Teachers' Federation.

Fullan, M. & Stiegelbauer, S. (1991). *The new meaning of educational change.* New York: Teachers College Press.

Glatthorn, A.A. (1990). Cooperative professional development: Facilitating the growth of the special education teacher and the classroom teacher. *Remedial and Special Education, 11* (3), 29-34.

Gordon, T. (1977). *Leadership effectiveness training (L.E.T.): The no-lose way to release the production potential in people.* Toronto: Bantam.

Heese, R.F. & Tepper, D.T. (1972). Nonverbal components of empathic communication. *Journal of Counseling Psychology, 19,* 417-424.

Idol, L., Paolucci-Whitcomb, P., & Nevin, A. (1986). *Collaborative consultation.* Austin, TX: Pro-Ed.

Jackson, P. (1968). *Life in classrooms.* New York: Holt, Rinehart and Winston.

Johnson, D., Johnson, R., Holubec, E.J., & Roy, D. (1984). *Circles of learning.* Washington, DC: Association for Supervision and Curriculum Development.

Kagan, S. (1990) *Cooperative learning.* San Juan Capistrano, CA: Resources for Teachers.

Kriegel, R.J. & Patler, L. (1991). *If it ain't broke . . . break it!* New York: Warner.

Kubler-Ross, E. (1969). *On death and dying.* New York: Macmillan.

Maslow, A.H. (1970). *Motivation and personality.* New York: Harper and Row.

Mehrabian, A. (1971). Nonverbal betrayal of feeling. *Journal of Experimental Research in Personality, 5,* 64-73.

Merrill, D.W. & Reid, R.H. (1981). *Personal styles and effective performance.* Radnor, PA: Chilton.

Meyers, J., Parsons, R.D., & Martin, R. (1979). *Mental health consultation in the schools: A comprehensive guide for psychologists, social workers, psychiatrists, counselors, educators, and other human services professionals.* San Francisco: Jossey-Bass.

Phillips, V. & McCullough, L. (1990). Consultation-based programming: Instituting the collaborative ethic in schools. *Exceptional Children, 56*(4), 291-304.

Phillips, V. & McCullough, L. (1993). *Student/staff support teams.* Longmont, CO: Sopris West.

Pugach, M.C. & Johnson, L.J. (1988a). Rethinking the relationship between consultation and collaborative problem-solving [special issue]. *Focus on Exceptional Children, 21*(4).

Pugach, M.C. & Johnson, L.J. (1988b) Peer collaboration: Helping teachers help themselves. *Teaching Exceptional Children, 20*(3), 75-77.

Pugach, M.C. & Johnson, L.J. (1988c). Peer collaboration: Enhancing teacher problem-solving capabilities for students at risk. Paper presented at the Annual Meeting of the American Educational Research Association, New Orleans. (ERIC Document Reproduction Service No. SP 030114)

Rosenfield, S. (1987). *Instructional consultation*. Hillsdale, NJ: Lawrence Erlbaum Associates.

Sarason, S. (1990). *The predictable failure of school reform: Can we change the course before it is too late?* San Francisco: Jossey-Bass.

Schein, E.H. (1969). *Process consultation: Its role in organizational development*. Reading, MA: Addison-Wesley.

Sculley, J. (1987). *Odyssey: Pepsi to Apple*. New York: Harper and Row.

Sparks, D. (1992). Becoming an authentic consultant: An interview with Peter Block. *Staff Development, 13* (2), 12.

Tharp, R.G. & Wetzel, R.J. (1969). *Behavior modification in the natural environment*. New York: Academic Press.

West, J.F. & Idol, L. (1990). Collaborative consultation in the education of mildly handicapped and at-risk students. *Remedial and Special Education, 11*(1), 22-31.

Aldinger, L., Warger, C., & Eavy, P. *Strategies for teacher collaboration.* Ann Arbor, MI: Exceptional Innovations.

Allington, R. & Broikou, K. (1988). Development of shared knowledge: A new role for classroom and specialist teachers. *The Reading Teacher, 41*(8), 806-811.

Barnabus, B. (1971). *Develop your power to deal with people.* West Nyack, NY: Parker.

Beck, R. & Williamson, R. (Eds.). (1990). *Project RIDE: Responding to individual differences in education.* Longmont, CO: Sopris West.

Beier, E.G. & Evans, G.V. (1975). *People readings: How we control others, how they control us.* New York: Warner.

Bergan, J.R. (1977). *Behavioral consultation.* Columbus, OH: Merrill.

Block, P. (1981). *Flawless consulting.* Austin, TX: Learning Concepts.

Bolton, R. (1986). *People skills: How to assert yourself, listen to others, and resolve conflicts.* NY: Simon and Schuster.

Bramson, R.M. (1981). *Coping with difficult people.* Garden City, NY: Doubleday.

Brandt, R.S. (1987). On cooperation in schools: A conversation with David and Roger Johnson. *Educational Leadership, 45*(3), 14-19.

Bristol, C.M. (1969). *The magic of believing.* New York: Pocket Books.

Brown, D. & Schulte, A.C. (1987). A social learning model of consultation. *Professional Psychology: Research and Practice, 18,* 283-287.

Brown, D., Pryzwansky, W., & Shulte, A. (1987). *Psychological consultation.* Boston: Allyn and Bacon.

Brown, D., Wyne, M.D., Blackburn, J.E., & Powel, W.C. (1979). *Consultation: Strategy for improving education.* Boston: Allyn and Bacon.

Buscaglia, L. (1986). *Loving each other: The challenge of human relationships.* Westminister, MD: Fawcett.

Caplan, G. (1970). *The theory and practice of mental health consultation.* New York: Basic Books.

Carkhuff, R.R. (1973a). *The art of helping.* Amherst, MA: Human Resource Development Press.

Carkhuff, R.R. (1973b). *The art of problem solving.* Amherst, MA: Human Resource Development Press.

Carkhuff, R.R. (1983). *Interpersonal skills and human productivity.* Amherst, MA: Human Resource Development Press.

Chandler, L.A. (1980). Consultative services in the schools: A model. *Journal of School Psychology, 18*(4), 399-401.

Conoley, J.C. & Conoley, C.W. (1982). *School consultation: A guide to practice and training.* New York: Pergamon Press.

Curtis, M.J. & Zins, J.E. (Eds.). (1981). *The theory and practice of school consultation.* Springfield, IL: Thomas.

Dettmar, D., Thurston, L., & Dyck, N. (1993). *Consultation, collaboration, and teamwork for students with special needs.* Boston: Allyn and Bacon.

Dettmer, P. (1989). The consulting teacher in programs for gifted and talented students. *Arkansas Gifted Education Magazine, 3*(2), 4-7.

Dyck, N. & Dettmer, P. (1989). Collaborative consultation: A promising tool for serving gifted learning-disabled students. *Journal of Reading, Writing, and Learning Disabilities, 5*(3), 253-264.

Egan, G. (1982). *The skilled helper* (2nd ed.). Monterey, CA: Brooks/Cole.

Evans, S. (1980). The consultant role of the resource teacher. *Exceptional Children, 46*, 402-403.

Fisher, R. & Brown, S. (1988). *Getting together: Building relationships as we negotiate.* NY: Penguin.

Friend, M. (1984). Consultation skills for resource teachers. *Learning Disability Quarterly, 7*, 246-250.

Friend, M. & Bauwens, J. (1988). Managing resistance: An essential consulting skill for learning disabilities teachers. *Journal of Learning Disabilities, 21*, 556-561.

Friend, M. & Cook, L. (1990). Collaboration as a predictor for success in school reform. *Journal of Educational and Psychological Consultation, 1* (1), 69-86.

Friend, M. & Bauwens, J. (1988). Managing resistance: An essential consulting skill for learning disabilities teachers. *Journal of Learning Disabilities, 21*, 556-561.

Gallessich, J. (1973). Organizational factors influencing consultation in schools. *Journal of School Psychology, 11*(1), 57-65.

Gallessich, J. (1974). Training the school psychologist for consultation. *Journal of School Psychology, 12*, 138-149.

Gallessich, J. (1982). *The profession and practice of consultation.* San Francisco: Jossey-Bass.

Gawain, S. (1982). *Creative visualization.* New York: Bantam.

Gersten, R., Darch, C., Davis, G., & George, N. (1991). Apprentice-ship and intensive training of consulting teachers: A naturalistic study. *Exceptional Children*, 57(3), 226-237.

Gould, R.L. (1978). *Transformations: Growth and change in adult life.* New York: Touchstone.

Grinder, J. & Bandler, R. (1976). *The structure of magic II.* Palo Alto, CA: Science and Behavior Books.

Hall, G.E. & Hord, S.M. (1987). *Change in schools: Facilitating the process.* Albany, NY: State University of New York.

Heron, T.E. & Harris, K. (1987). *The educational consultant.* Austin, TX: Pro-Ed.

Hord, S., Rutherford, W., Huling-Austin, L. & Hall, G. (1987). *Taking charge of change.* Alexandria, VA: Association for Supervision and Curriculum Development.

Huefner, D. (1988). The consulting teacher model: Risks and opportunities. *Exceptional Children*, 54(5), 403-414.

Hughs, J. & Falk, R. (1981). Resistance, reactance, and consultation. *Journal of School Psychology*, 19(2), 139-142.

Idol, L. (1990). The scientific art of classroom consultation. *Journal of Educational and Psychological Consultation*, 1(1), 3-22.

Jackson, P. (1968). *Life in classrooms.* New York: Holt, Rinehart and Winston.

Jersild, A.T. (1955). *When teachers face themselves.* New York: Teachers College Press.

Johnson, D.W. & Johnson, R.T. (1987a). *Joining together: Group theory and group skills* (3rd ed.). Englewood Cliffs, NJ: Prentice Hall.

Johnson, D.W. & Johnson, R.T. (1987b). Research showing the benefits of adult cooperation. *Educational Leadership*, 45(3), 27-30.

Journal of Psychological Type (formerly named *Research in Psychological Type*). All issues.

Joyce, B. & Showers, B. (1987). Low-cost arrangements for peer coaching. *Journal of Staff Development, 8,* 22-24.

Joyce, B. & Showers, B. (1988). *Student achievement through staff development.* New York: Longman.

Jung, C.G. (1923). *Psychological types.* New York: Harcourt Brace.

Keirsey, D. & Bates, M. (1978). *Please understand me.* Del Mar, CA: Prometheus Nemesis.

Knackendoffel, E.A., Robinson, S.M., Deshler, D.D., & Schumaker, J.B. (1992). *Collaborative problem solving.* Lawrence, KS: Edge Enterprises.

Kroth, R. & Scholl, G. (1978). *Getting schools involved with parents.* Arlington, VA: Council for Exceptional Children.

Kummerow, J.M. & McAllister, L.W. (1988). Team-building with the Myers-Briggs type indicator: Case studies. *Journal of Psychological Type, 15,* 26-32.

Lawrence, G. (1982). *People types and tiger stripes: A practical guide to learning styles.* King of Prussia, PA: Center for Applied Psychology.

Lewis, A. (1993). *Leadership styles.* Arlington, VA: American Association of School Administrators.

Lieberman, A. (1986). Collaborative work. *Educational Leadership, 43*(5), 4-8.

Lieberman, A. & Miller, L. (1984). *Teachers, their world, and their work.* Alexandria, VA: Association for Supervision and Curriculum Development.

Lippitt, G. & Lippitt, R. (1978). *The consulting process in action.* La Jolla, CA: University Associates.

Loucks-Horsley, S., Harding, C.K., Arbuckle, M.A., Murray, L.B., Dubea, C., & Williams, M.K. (1987). *Continuing to learn: A guidebook for teacher development.* Andover, MA: The Regional Laboratory for Educational Improvement of the Northeast and Islands.

Mehrabian, A. (1971). Nonverbal betrayal of feeling. *Journal of Experimental Research in Personality, 5,* 64-73.

Morsink, C.V., Thomas, C.C., & Correa, V.I. (1991). *Interactive teaming: Consultation and collaboration in special programs.* Columbus, OH: Merrill.

Nevin, A., Thousand, J., & Paolucci-Whitcomb, P. (1990). Collaborative consultation: Empowering public school personnel to provide heterogeneous schooling for all—or, who rang that bell? *Journal of Educational and Psychological Consultation,* 1(1), 41-67.

Parsons, R. & Meyers, J. (1984). *Developing consultation skills.* San Francisco: Jossey-Bass.

Piersel, W.D. & Gutkin, T.B. (1983). Resistance to school-based consultation: A behavioral analysis of the problem. *Psychology in the Schools, 20,* 311-326.

Polsgrove, L. & McNeil, M. (1989). The consultation process: Research and practice. *Remedial and Special Education, 10*(1), 6-13, 20.

Pryzwansky, W.B. & White, G.W. (1983). The influence of consultee characteristics on preferences for consultation approaches. *Professional Psychology, 14,* 457-464.

Pugach, M.C. (1988). The consulting teacher in the context of educational reform. *Exceptional Children, 55*(3), 273-275.

Pugach, M.C. & Johnson, L.J. (1989). The challenge of implementing collaboration between general and special education. *Exceptional Children, 56*(3), 232-235.

Pugach, M.C. & Johnson, L.J. (1990). Fostering the continued democratization of consultation through action research. *Teacher Education and Special Education, 13*(3-4), 240-245.

Reinking, R.H., Livesay, G., & Kohl, M. (1978). The effects of consultation style on consultee productivity. *American Journal of Community Psychology, 6,* 283-290.

Reisberg, L. & Wolf, R. (1986). Developing a consulting program in special education: Implementation and interventions. *Focus on Exceptional Children, 19*, 1-14.

Robert, M. (1973). *Loneliness in the schools: What to do about it.* Niles, IL: Argus Communication.

Sarason, S.B. (1982). *The culture of the school and the problem of change* (2nd ed.). Boston: Allyn and Bacon.

Schein, E. (1978). The role of the consultant: Content expert or process facilitator? [special issue] *Personnel and Guidance Journal, 56* (6 & 7).

Schein, E.H. (1969). *Process consultation: Its role in organizational development.* Reading, MA: Addison-Wesley.

Schon, D. (1987). *Educating the reflective practitioner.* San Francisco: Jossey-Bass.

Schuck, J. (1979). The parent-professional partnership: Myth or realty? *Education Unlimited, 1*(4), 26-28.

Simpson, G.W. (1990). Keeping it alive: Elements of school culture that sustain innovation. *Educational Leadership, 47*(8), 34-37.

Tindel, G.A. & Taylor-Pendergast, S. (1989). A taxonomy for objectively analyzing the consultation process. *Remedial and Special Education, 10*(2), 6-16.

Walton, R.E. (1969). *Interpersonal peacemaking: confrontations and third-part consultation.* Reading, MA: Addision Wesley.

Wanges, R.D. (1979). Teacher responses to collaborative consultation. *Psychology in the Schools, 16*, 127-131.

West, I.F., Idol, L., & Cannon, G. (1988). *Collaboration in the schools: Communicating interacting, and problem solving.* Austin, TX: Pro-Ed.

West, J.F. (1990). Educational collaboration in the restructuring of schools. *Journal of Educational and Psychological Consultation, 1*(1), 23-40.

West, J.F. & Cannon, G.S. (1988). Essential collaborative consultant competencies for regular and special educators. *Journal of Learning Disabilities, 21* (1), 56-63.